Dark of Night in the Light of Day:
The Art of Interpreting Your Dreams
By Karen Frazier

ISBN-13: 978-0692938157 (Afterlife Publishing)

ISBN-10: 069293815X

For dreamers everywhere

Foreword: The Power of Dreams

My dreams are always so vivid and "real" … sometimes fun, sometimes happy, sometimes downright terrifying. Why do I have recurring dreams about being able to fly, running away from Frankenstein, my teeth falling out, dodging tornadoes, and falling from high places? What about dreams that are prophetic or dreams that include friends from long ago, deceased love ones, or that one dream where I have a final test to take in school but then realize I've missed the entire semester of classes and don't know any of the required material?

Sometimes dreams are amazing. Other times they are exhausting. But why do we dream at all? Certainly for more than entertainment's sake, right? For more than stress relief? Dreams have to mean something more profound?

To answer this question as a teenager, I grabbed my mom's dream interpretation book off the bookshelf and was immediately intrigued with just how complex the subconscious mind is, just how much it reveals to us when we least expect it. The mind is always hard at work inputting, processing, deciphering, including while we dream.

Today, more than 30 years after picking up that first dream interpretation book, my interest in dreams remains as strong as ever. In fact, a few years ago, I mentioned to a friend, Karen Frazier, that I wanted to start a dream interpretation column in my magazine, *Paranormal Underground*. Luckily for me and our readers, Karen volunteered to write the column.

Reader reactions to Karen's interpretations have ranged from "amazing" to "now it all makes complete sense" to "incredibly insightful." Another reader shared with us that Karen's dream interpretation helped set them on an entirely new life path, one they felt destined to explore. One particularly excited reader said, "Karen hit the nail on the head. Her interpretation accurately reflected events going on in my life right now. It's really incredible."

Thanks to reader feedback, we see the impact and power of dream interpretation and how each dream analysis provides personal insights that open up new perspectives. Other reactions to Karen's interpretations have included: "I hope you continue helping others like me" and "the insights Karen provided allowed me to better grasp things I needed to pay attention to in my life."

Karen has also interpreted many dreams for me, personally. One of the first dreams I sent to Karen for interpretation seemed so incoherent and bizarre I thought it could not be interpreted at all. After Karen's interpretation, however, I had an "a-ha moment" where some deep-rooted issues surfaced, and I was finally able to come to terms with life struggles that had been perplexing me.

In another interpretation, Karen brought to light how the symbols, numbers, and participants in my dream reflected how my spiritual side was struggling with my ego on some very personal predicaments. These and many other interpretations Karen has done for me allowed me to get beyond hang-ups and roadblocks I wasn't able to see in my waking life.

The above examples just scratch the surface of the power of dream interpretation. Dreams do help us decipher everything from subconscious anxieties to passing insecurities to deep-seated dilemmas. I encourage you to use Karen's Dream Interpretation Worksheet at the end of this book to begin deciphering and understanding your own dreams. The process is an eye-opening experience that allows for invaluable spiritual understanding and guidance.

—Cheryl Knight, Editor
Paranormal Underground magazine

Quick Start Guide to Interpreting Your Dreams

Step 1: Note what you think the dream means.

Step 2: Determine the dream's context or setting and what it represents.

Step 3: Notice the people in the dream and what they represent.

Step 4: List any numbers and their meanings.

Step 5: List any colors and their meanings.

Step 6: List any shapes that stand out and their meanings.

Step 7: List other symbols and their meanings.

Step 8: Use the plot to put the entire dream together.

Introduction

I've always had a rich dream life. Every night, my sleep is filled with vivid imagery that sometimes stays on my mind for hours or days after I wake. Other times, I wake knowing I've experienced something significant, but the dream fades almost instantly and I'm left with a vague feeling there's something important I need to remember.

Even as a child, my dreams were filled with memorable images, sweeping adventures, and complex plots. They were rich with people, animals, bright colors, and plenty of action. Some were so vivid, they seemed even more real than my waking life. Others had an otherworldly quality and elements so bizarre it left me scratching my head.

Throughout my life, my dreams have enriched and informed me. When I was pregnant with my son, I dreamed of him before he was born and on the day of his birth, the baby I held in my arms was the one I had seen in my dreams over and over again. When I was in my 20s and my life felt out of control, I had a recurring dream about riding in a car racing down a hill with a lake at the bottom and brakes that didn't work.

I also used to dream frequently about two different types of disasters: earthquakes and train derailments. Always within 24 hours, one of those two events would occur somewhere in the world. Because of this, I knew at an early age my dreams were trying to tell me something. Sometimes, it was easy to decipher. Other times, it was a mystery.

I started journaling my dreams as a young adult, looking for common themes to see how they fit within the context of my life. Because of my fascination with dreams, I familiarized myself with the works of Carl Jung, who described the collective unconscious, and I studied the words of Edgar Cayce, who provided guidelines for working with dreams.

I was fascinated by what I learned about myself and how accurate the imagery from my dreams actually was, and I started sharing what I'd learned with close friends. Some of those friends began asking me to help them understand their own dreams, as well. Then a few years ago, I started writing a dream interpretation column for *Paranormal Underground Magazine* where readers wrote in with their dreams, and I interpreted them. I received feedback from many readers about how uncannily accurate the interpretations were, and many shared they were able to work through issues in their lives because of the dream interpretations.

That's why I'm offering this book. Many people have expressed fascination about what their dreams mean, and I lack the time interpret them all. Several people have asked me to write this book, and my response was always, "The world doesn't need yet another dream symbol dictionary." I stand by that belief. There are many excellent resources that will tell you everything you need to know about various dream symbols. So, for me to tread on that territory would be a rehashing of information that's already out there; it wouldn't offer anything new.

However, I realized there is a way I can help: I can offer you the tools for interpreting your own dreams because your insight into yourself is always going to be keener than my insight into you, and a big part of dream interpretation is filtering things through your own personal symbolism.

With that in mind, this book offers framework for interpreting dreams. It provides a roadmap to interpreting your own dreams, offering information about how to remember them, what to notice and record about them, and how to place the information you receive into the context of your life. Then, it provides worksheets that allow you to do this with your own dreams. Throughout, I share my interpretations of dreams people have sent to me over the years so you can see the process in action.

I hope you find this book a helpful resource as you delve into the world of your dreams. I suggest using a good dream dictionary as a companion to this book; online I recommend DreamMoods.com, which is one of the best internet resources I've found. When working with a dictionary, you'll find several interpretations for each dream symbol. Choose those that make the most sense to you. It requires discernment, but with more practice you'll find it gets easier to understand your dreams even without going through the entire rigmarole of interpretation. And if you wind up in a pinch or need a little extra insight, feel free to email your dreams to editor@paranormalunderground.net (you can request that they be anonymous), and they may wind up in my column.

Karen Frazier
Chehalis, WA
August 12, 2017

Hi Karen:

There was a beautiful pit bull, a light tan color. He was apparently vicious so my husband shot him. But he wouldn't die so my husband shot him several times. Then he called the police. There was also a baby, maybe a year or two old. Something was apparently wrong with her too, so we decided she also had to be shot. She wouldn't die either. She never cried or made a sound. She just reached for me to hold her. When I looked at the wound, it was her leg. That's odd because my husband used to shoot competitively. He doesn't miss. I asked why he shot her leg, but he didn't answer. I cried because I didn't want the baby or the dog to suffer. I wanted to keep her and take her to the doctor, but my husband said we couldn't take her or he'd have to explain why he shot her. He was worried about what would happen when the police got there. As a side note, I have no idea who the baby was. It's like she was a stray like the dog. It was a really disturbing dream.

~Anonymous

Hello:

Thanks for sharing your dream with me. It has several important symbols.

- A pit bull suggests you are feeling defensive.
- A vicious dog symbolizes inner conflict.
- The color tan symbolizes neutrality.
- Shooting symbolizes hidden or not so hidden aggressive feelings.
- Police represent control and authority.
- A baby symbolizes innocence, new beginnings – or it may be a representation of the Divine Child archetype.
- A wound represents grief and distress.
- Legs represent standing up for yourself.

First, I'll start by saying your husband in your dream is probably a representation of how you feel about him on some deep level. The dog and baby, however, are aspects of yourself. So the dog is a vicious pit bull. As this is some deeply-rooted aspect of yourself, it suggests you are in a position of defensiveness and inner conflict, although the dog's color, which is tan, is a neutral color, so it suggests you may be covering the inner conflict with a more neutral-appearing stance, even though that isn't really how you feel.

Your husband is shooting at the dog, which suggests you see him as aggressive, particularly in relation to your own defensiveness or inner conflict. He's also shooting the baby, which is another aspect of you – your innocence and hope for new beginnings. In other words, I think you have some hopes and wishes, but you feel your husband's aggression may keep you from expressing them.

It's interesting you are complicit in shooting the baby – you say "we decided," suggesting you feel you are participating in or allowing the wounds your husband is inflicting – perhaps by not standing up for yourself as you feel you should. However, the fact both the dog and the baby won't die suggests a tenacity in you to follow your own truth and hopes, no matter what. It's also interesting you ask your husband why he shot the baby; this suggests you are bewildered about his treatment of you. Him not answering tells me he's not giving you any clues or you're not able to make sense of why his behavior is as it is. I'm wondering from this small part of the dream if your husband's behavior changed towards you recently (or since you married him) and that is part of what is confusing you.

You say your husband called the police about the dog. It's significant he did, because it shows you feel he is exerting some type of power or authority over you. He won't call the police about the baby, however. You feel he doesn't want these new hopes you have to come to light to give them power and authority, as well.

A wound on the baby's leg is significant. The leg symbolizes your base of support and standing up for yourself. The wounded leg suggests you are feeling grief or distress at what you see as your husband trying to keep you from standing up for yourself.

The dream suggests you are feeling conflict within your relationship, and you are distressed about your husband's controlling nature. If you feel emotionally safe with your husband (and the dream suggests you may not), I recommend sitting down with him and discussing how you feel, as well as how his actions and aggression make you feel. Open communication, if it is safe to do so, is key to resolving conflict. If you don't feel safe having such a conversation, it may be time to take a deeper look at your relationship and consider pursuing individual or couples counseling.

~Karen

Chapter 1 – Your Dreams and Why They Matter

The concept of dream interpretation isn't new. It's been around for thousands of years spanning multiple civilizations; you'll find examples of it extending into antiquity, such as a description of dream interpretation in the *Epic of Gilgamesh* from ancient Babylon. Hieroglyphics from ancient Egypt show depictions of dreams, as well as their interpretation. Ancient Greeks believed dreams could be prophetic and healing.

In literature, authors describe character's dreams as a device to provide readers better insight into the character's psyche. Christians believe God communicates with them via dreams. In the Muslim faith, it is believed dreams come from three sources: the body, the mind, and the soul as it travels through the other world.

In modern times, the belief dreams can convey significant information crosses both international and philosophical borders. More than half of Americans believe dreams provide symbolic and significant information, for example, while nearly three-quarters of people in India do (Morewedge and Norton, 2009)[i].

What Are Dreams?

Researchers at the University of California at Santa Cruz (UCSC)[ii] list the following four criteria in their definition of a dream:

- A dream is a form of thinking that occurs when the ego (the "I" or sense of self) shuts down, external stimuli are blocked, and there is a certain level of brain activity (i.e. when you're asleep or unconscious);
- Dreams are experienced, as opposed to viewed, because they impart sensory data and evoke emotions;
- The dream is what you remember upon waking, so what you notice as a dream is actually a memory of the experience of the dream;
- The dream is your written or spoken report of the experience of the memory.

In other words, while you experience dreams when you sleep, the memory of the experience and the spoken or written word is what we're discussing here in this book as we talk about them.

Dreams occur during a cycle of sleep known as rapid-eye movement (REM), and most people have an average of four to six dreams per night, according to the National Sleep Foundation[iii]. In an average eight hours of sleep, you might spend two of those hours dreaming.

What if I Don't Dream?

Everyone dreams, even you. However, the National Sleep Foundation suggests people forget as much as 99 percent of their dreams, which is why you might wake up in the morning and feel as if you've spent a dreamless night. Many people, me included, have had the experience of waking from a dream and watching it fade right before our eyes until we don't remember any details at all. This is because dreams can be ephemeral, and unless you make a point of remembering and recording them, they are likely to fade away. Of course, this isn't the case with all dreams; some are so vivid or arresting they linger long after you wake. I have some dreams from childhood I can still recall clearly.

Why Do They Matter?

If dreams were merely nonsense, then their content wouldn't matter except as a form of nighttime entertainment to keep your mind busy while you slept. And indeed, some dreams are exactly that...your mind processing parts of your day and storing it in your memory. Other dreams, however, may have greater significance.

Many psychologists have suggested dreaming can provide you insight into your psyche, while metaphysicians and spiritual scholars posit dreams may provide important information about the state of your soul, your life's path, and more.

Psychological Theories of Dreaming – Freud, Jung, and Hall

Sigmund Freud[iv] theorized dreams were expressions of unconscious or forbidden desires and motivations. Therefore, Freud believed, dreams offered insight into these desires and motivations, providing a path to the subconscious or unconscious. Freud believed dreams provided information about repressed thoughts and beliefs that were somewhat distorted from reality but still offered valuable insight into his subjects. In fact, Freud based his entire theory and approach on a dream he had when he was worried about a patient and feeling guilty she was not doing well. From that dream, Freud recognized how his own subconscious feelings and desires resulted in his dream as a form of wish fulfillment, which he then transferred to his therapeutic work with patients. Freud believed symbols from dreams came from the personal unconscious, which is personal symbolism significant only to the dreamer.

While Carl Jung[v] found Freud's theories of dream interpretation interesting, he felt the theory was limited in its scope and therefore lacking when used as a therapeutic model. A brilliant psychoanalyst himself, Jung developed his own theory of dream interpretation which laid a foundation for modern forms of the art. Jung believed dreams were highly symbolic, and when those symbols were observed and translated using both personal unconscious symbolism and symbols from the collective consciousness (a.k.a. collective unconsciousness – I'll use the terms interchangeably) which is a shared set of beliefs, ideas, and symbols that may occur among a group of people, such as a society, a family, or all of humanity, one could discover the true meaning of the dream.

In Freud's approach if symbols appeared in dreams, it shows only the dreamer's personal symbolism. In Jung's approach, symbols may be personal but might also arise from the collective consciousness, such as via archetypes or numerology, among many other symbol sets. Jung also believed that, while collective unconscious symbolism may come into play, in the end the symbolism even from the collective unconsciousness wound up being deeply personal to the dreamer because dreams needed to be interpreted in the context of the dreamer's waking experiences, thoughts, beliefs, and other psychological factors.

Psychologist Calvin S. Hall Jr.[vi] formed his own theory of dreams as a cognitive process providing insight into the unconscious mind. Hall believed you could interpret dreams based on a quantitative coding system he created from analysis of thousands of recorded dreams. According to Hall, in order to interpret dreams one must know the actions of the dreamer in the dream, the objects in the dream, the dreamer's interaction within the dream with others, and the dream's setting. Knowing these things will help you understand the dreamer, not the dream.

Metaphysical Approach – Edgar Cayce

Psychic Edgar Cayce[vii] also played a role in creating a framework for interpreting dreams. Cayce took a practical approach, sidestepping most of the psychoanalysis and offering a framework that allowed the layperson to interpret his or her own dreams.

Cayce based his approach on the individual's innate and intuitive knowledge of himself or herself, something that often came via the subconscious during the dream state. According to Cayce, dreams did more than offer psychological insight into the dreamer, they provided important information about the totality of the dreamer; body, mind, and spirit.

Cayce believed every person knew far more about himself on a subconscious level than he was aware of on a conscious level. Therefore, dreams served as intuitive information coming from levels of higher or deeper consciousness. Cayce also believed everything that occurred in one's life was foreshadowed in his or her dreams. Therefore, he saw great value in remembering one's dreams and discovering their meaning.

According to Cayce, dreams could tell the dreamer anything he or she needed to know, such as higher truths, relationship dynamics that needed to be addressed, physical illnesses, roadblocks to success, hidden dangers on the road of life, and many other subjects.

Cayce developed his own dream dictionary with common dream symbols (from the collective unconscious) for interpretation. You'll find Cayce's dream symbols in many dream dictionaries.

The State of Dream Interpretation Today

Today, you'll find all of the psychological theories of dream interpretation in full swing in therapeutic settings. Dream interpretation can prove invaluable in providing psychological insight. However, it also hit its stride as a means of learning more about yourself, and dreamers seeking more information about various aspects of self gain valuable insight by interpreting their dreams.

In spiritual and metaphysical fields, as well as in dream interpretation for personal insight, you'll find a combination of all of the above approaches. I view each as a tool you can use to gain greater insight into your dreams, and the method I describe in this book borrows from various theories and applications of dream interpretation in order to help you find a personalized approach that is the most meaningful to you.

Zeroing in on Your Dreams

As previously mentioned, people tend to forget about 95 to 99 percent of their dreams. If a dream is simply processing and storing memories, there's probably no need to remember it, but what about the dreams that provide significant information? How can you better remember them if you are someone prone to forgetting your dreams the second you open your eyes in the morning?

- Ask for a dream before you go to sleep. You can be specific and ask that the dream provide insight into a certain situation, or you can say, "Tell me what I need to know." Asking sets the intention you will have meaningful dreams, which is one of the best ways I know to begin to explore them.
- Set the intention you will remember your dreams upon waking before you fall asleep.
- Record your dream as soon as you wake from it. Some people keep a dream journal, a pen, and a small book light next to their bed so they can record it right away. Others keep a voice recorder (or a cell phone with a voice recording app) next to the bed and record the dream into that. Barring either of those items, you can also repeat the dream to yourself once or twice, which should help you remember it.

You are also more likely to remember you dreams if you don't drink alcohol or take medications (including herbal remedies) to help you sleep and if you are sleeping enough each night so you wake feeling well-rested.

[i] Morewedge, Carey K.; Norton, Michael I. "When dreaming is believing: The (motivated) interpretation of dreams.". Journal of Personality and Social Psychology. 96(2): 249–264. PMID 19159131. doi:10.1037/a0013264.

[ii] Schneider, Adam, and G William Domhoff. "Dreams FAQ." Dreams: FAQ, University of California at Santa Barbara, www2.ucsc.edu/dreams/FAQ/.

[iii] Russo, Lucy. "How Often Do We Dream." Sleep.org, National Sleep Foundation, 24 Oct. 2014, sleep.org/articles/how-often-dreams/.

[iv] McLeod, Saul. "Saul McLeod." Simply Psychology, Simply Psychology, 1 Jan. 1970, www.simplypsychology.org/Sigmund-Freud.html.

[v] Hurd, Ryan. "The Dream Theories of Carl Jung." Dream Studies Portal, Dream Studies Press, dreamstudies.org/2009/11/25/carl-jung-dream-interpretation/.

[vi] Domhoff, G. William, and Adam Schneider. "Calvin Hall." DreamResearch.org, University of California at Santa Barbara, www2.ucsc.edu/dreams/About/calvin.html.

[vii] "Insights from Dreams." Edgar Cayce's A.R.E, www.edgarcayce.org/the-readings/dreams/insights-from-dreams/.

Dreams from Readers

Dear Karen:

I dreamed was a nurse at a hospital. I came to work and put on my scrubs in the locker room. The scrubs were a dirty green, and I also put on a plastic butcher's apron. I put my stethoscope around my neck – not to my ears, but looped around the back with the earpieces hanging down on one side and the listening part on the other. I went to the ward where I was supposed to work and there was another nurse there in tidy, forest green scrubs. Suddenly, I felt really dirty and disheveled compared to how neatly turned out the other nurse(es) were. I wanted to change and get the right scrubs, but something (can't remember what) prevented that.

~Anonymous

Hi!

Thanks for allowing me to interpret your dream. There are several symbols present.

- The dream takes place in a hospital, which is the context of the dream. Hospitals in dreams represent healing, so this dream is about healing or health.
- In the dream you are a nurse, suggesting the aspect of yourself that is a healer.
- A locker room represents taking time or finding a place to calm down and cool off.
- Scrubs represent the desire to clean up your act.
- The color green represents health and positive changes, but the fact it is a muddy green color may suggest some ambivalence about these changes.
- An apron represents protection and secrecy.
- A stethoscope represents listening; however, you mention you aren't using it to listen, suggesting you may be unwilling to hear a message right now.
- The nurse (healer) in scrubs that are a clearer green than yours suggests you are feeling inadequate as far as healing goes, but you want to change that. Being unable to change your scrubs suggests you feel something is preventing you from doing so.

So pulling it all together, it seems your dream is suggesting you either wish to become a healer or are trying to heal some aspect of yourself, but you feel something is preventing you from doing that. You are either not hearing the information you are receiving or hearing/interpreting it incorrectly (in a way that doesn't serve you), and you are being overly self-protective (which may be the issue). This is making you feel unworthy, but you want to change. Pay attention to your intuition and try not to filter it through preconceived notions or beliefs about yourself.

~Karen

Chapter 2 –Types of Dreams

Not all dreams are created equal. Some are rich, vivid, and detailed. Some are short and lacking detail. Some make sense. Others don't. Some are nightmares, and some recur. Some leave you feeling happy and uplifted; others leave you angry or afraid. There are as many types of dreams as there are dreamers, but there are some common types you may experience.

Memory Processing/Consolidation

One common type of dream is memory processing and consolidation. This is your brain doing its housekeeping while you sleep – a sort of computer defrag of your memories. During this time, your brain may move memories from short to long term storage. These dreams often contain events from your day, and you are unlikely to remember them for long since they are mundane and don't have any "wow" factor. These dreams are not symbolic but are simply your brain cleaning up after a long day of making memories.

Repressed Memory Dreams

These dreams are often vivid and almost hyper-real. In them, you are yourself, typically a younger version of yourself, and you may be having an experience you don't remember. However when you wake, the dream stays with you because of how real it is.

A reader sent a dream I believe was a repressed memory. In it, the dreamer described himself in vivid detail as a little boy. He described the pajamas he wore and how they felt against his skin, the way the air felt and smelled, the scrape of a chair as he dragged it to the kitchen sink so he could stand on it and look out the window, the ticking of a kitchen clock echoing throughout the room, and a vivid scene he saw in his backyard as he stood on the chair. The extensive level of detail and the sensory reality of the dream convinced me it was likely a repressed memory, something that when I suggested it to the dreamer, he agreed it likely was although he had no recollection of such an incident.

Visitation Dreams

Last summer, I started having vivid dreams about one of my friend's husbands. I hadn't seen him in 30 years (they separated for years before getting back together a few years ago) although I'd kept in touch with my friend. He died suddenly shortly after they got back together. The dreams felt like real life; they had none of the elements of a typical dream. They were vivid, hyper-real, and I woke remembering every detail. He came to me several times that summer until I finally contacted my friend and told her about them. Turns out, many other people had been having similar dreams of her husband with the same hyper-real quality to them.

I believe these are visitation dreams, in which someone who has died comes back to communicate with you. I've had them about several people who have died, including my grandmother, a high school friend killed by a drunk driver, and a close family friend, and these dreams always have a different quality of hyper-reality. Sometimes, people mention feeling fear as they realize the person in the dream is dead, which often brings the dream to an immediate close.

I think these dreams occur because your loved ones who have died find it easiest to communicate with you when your defenses are down and your ego and conscious mind are disengaged. If you have these dreams, don't be afraid. Cherish them as what they are: messages of love from those who have passed.

Recurring Dreams

Many people have recurring dreams. Typically, these dreams are symbolic and often don't make much sense. Recurring dreams may be the exact same dream, it may be a recurring theme that keeps arising in a dream, or it may be one element of a dream that keeps coming up. I have a few of these from my own experience I can relate to you.

One recurring dream is exact every time I have it. In it, I am at school, it's finals week, and I haven't been to any of my classes, nor do I even know where the classroom is. This is a common anxiety dream, and I've had it since college. Many people have a similar version of this dream.

For many years, elevators that would not stop at my floor were a recurring setting of my dreams. The circumstances of the dream might change, as would people and other symbols, but that darn elevator that would never stop on my floor was always there. Elevator dreams are about moving upward in life – emotionally, spiritually, etc., and when it wouldn't stop at my floor, my dream was telling me something I thought I should be doing or experiencing wasn't actually on my path. When I loosened the reigns and started flowing more naturally with life, the dreams stopped.

I also have a recurring dream element: in this case a person. You'll see one dream with this element in it on the example Dream Interpretation Worksheet at the end of this book. The person is a kid who was in every class with me from kindergarten through high school. His name was Brad, and he lived a few blocks away. We were never particularly good friends although we were friendly, but he was a constant in a changing world just with his mere presence. Now, he shows up frequently in dreams. I started to notice that whenever Brad shows up in a dream, it foretells that something in my life is about to change drastically.

Prophetic Dreams

There is controversy about whether dreams can be prophetic. No research has proven dreams have a prophetic element, but there are plenty of people who share dreams they've had which later seemed to come true. Brad, who I described as an element in my dreams, is a prophetic symbol for me because he signifies change is on its way. I also have prophetic dreams about earthquakes and train derailments, as well as school shootings.

The problem I've always had with prophetic dreams (and a frustration others have professed, as well), is these dreams don't provide enough detail so I can do anything about it. For example, I may dream of a school shooting, but I see no details. Ditto for earthquakes and train wrecks. As you can imagine, this can be frustrating and painful, leaving me feeling helpless.

Recently, however, I've come up with something I can "do" about information received in prophetic dreams. I can send love and energy to the situation in hopes the energy can somehow alter it, or ease it for at least one soul. If you have prophetic dreams and feel equally helpless, I recommend trying this.

It may take a while for you to learn to recognize prophetic dreams. For me, they are about certain subjects, and they have a quality that differs from my other dreams, but I was only able to recognize those patterns after I'd had the dreams several times and then watched them play out in the real world. I suspect it will be similar for you, as well.

Lucid Dreams

Lucid dreaming is super cool, and beyond the scope of this book. In lucid dreaming, you are aware you're dreaming, and you can take control of elements of the dream, which then provides you the opportunity to have some dream fun. Entire books have been written on this subject, and if it's one that interests you, I recommend picking up a book and learning some techniques. You can recognize these dreams because you can control them.

Traveling Dreams

These dreams occur when you travel the astral plane while sleeping. Often, traveling dreams are lucid. You may be able to control them, or you may not. They will have a hyper-real quality to them, and you'll go places where you have vivid sensory experiences. During the dream, you may experience the sensation of being out of your body and floating, or you may feel embodied. They are characterized by the vivid sensory information you experience in your travels.

Dreams Related to Physical Discomfort (Fevers, Pain, Indigestion)

Ever had a fever dream? For me they are edgy, blurry, and uncomfortable. I can wake from a fever dream and go right back into it. Even if nothing particularly disturbing is happening, they feel disturbing. You probably know what your fever dreams feel like. They are generally not symbolic, but rather are a manifestation of your illness.

If you are in pain or some other type of physical discomfort, this may show up in your dreams, as well. For example, if you dream you have to go to the bathroom or you are going to the bathroom, you probably need to go to the bathroom. If you dream you're guzzling water, you might be really thirsty. Once while sharing a hotel bed with my older sister when we were kids, she punched me in the stomach. The pain showed up in my dream before I woke up and pulled her hair. She claims she was dreaming when she punched me. Forty years later, I still don't believe her.

Symbolic Dreams

The bulk of this book will discuss interpreting symbolic dreams. These dreams are usually a unique combination of things that seem to make sense and things that make no sense at all. Rapid and inexplicable scene changes often occur. You may have strange experiences. You may find yourself in familiar settings but doing odd things or seeing strange people. These weird dreams are usually the ones that provide the greatest insight and once you understand the symbols in the dream, they become a key that unlocks its meaning. Once unlocked, although the dream was weird, its meaning makes perfect sense.

Some Common Symbolic Dreams and Their Meanings

I mentioned one of my common dreams earlier – being in school and not having studied for my finals. This is one of many dreams common to a lot of people, and they tend to have a similar interpretation across the board. I suspect you'll recognize your own dreams in some of the dreams that follow.

School/Exams/Failing or Not Studying

I thought I was the only person in the world who had this dream until my dad told me he'd had virtually the same dream since he was in college. I asked around, and many other people report having this common dream, as well. The elements may vary from person to person, but essentially in the dream you are in high school or college and you are either failing your final exams, taking them and didn't study, or like me, didn't go to class for the entire semester so you have no idea where the classroom is or what might be on the test.

This is a common anxiety dream that is usually about work (although if you're still in school, it could be about school). The dream typically means you're afraid you aren't doing well at work, that you may be failing, or that you are afraid of being fired. It also may reflect a general lack of confidence in your job or studies.

Teeth Falling Out

Have you ever dreamed one or more of your teeth are falling out? You're not alone. This is a common dream, or it may be a common recurring element in dreams. These are typically dreams about anxiety, often about personal appearance or your ability to survive (you need to eat to live, if you have no teeth, eating is an issue).

Naked or Underwear

Gah – you're walking down a busy city street, and you're naked (or in your undies)! Being in your altogether in public in a dream is about your insecurities and vulnerabilities. Nakedness in dreams is a literal representation of just how vulnerable and exposed you are feeling about something. Likewise, you may feel like an imposter unable to do what you say you are doing (such as at your job – this is the commonly occurring imposter syndrome).

Trying to Run Away and You Can't Move

Is there any more helpless feeling in a dream than trying to run away from something threatening only to find your feet frozen to the ground or your muscles paralyzed so you can't move? Even worse, what if you can run, but only in slow motion? What gives with these dreams? Typically, they are about feelings of low self-confidence, either related to a particular situation or in general.

Falling

When I was a kid, there was a rumor that if you hit the ground in a falling dream, you would wake up dead. In other words, you wouldn't wake up from the dream. Once I hit the ground during one of these dreams, however, I was very relieved to wake up. Falling dreams are typically a warning from your subconscious there's something in your life you need to change or fix. The context and other symbols in the dream can give you more information.

Chase

Once in a dream, I was being chased by a black helicopter shooting lasers at me. It was terrifying! However, chase dreams are common stress dreams. The further context (in my case, a black helicopter and lasers) can give you insight into what is causing the stress.

Inability to Use Technology or Malfunctioning Technology

These might have confounded Jung or Freud, but technology has started to figure into our dreams because it is such a persistent part of our lives. Common dreams center around being unable to dial your iPhone or typing the wrong words into your computer, for instance. These are usually about communication and feeling like you are unable to communicate effectively.

Flying Dreams

Not all dream meanings are negative, and flying dreams are an excellent example of this. You usually wake from a flying dream feeling excited, happy, joyful, or inspired. Flying in dreams symbolizes your ability or desire to reach new heights.

Childbirth Dreams

These are more common in women than men, but men have them, as well. Dreams about giving birth to a baby are about creativity and nurturing, and bringing new energy and ideas into your life.

Driving Dreams

If you are driving a vehicle in your dreams, it symbolizes your life's path. If someone else is driving, you feel like someone else is controlling your destiny. You can discover more about these dreams by the other symbols in the dream.

Sex Dreams

While sometimes sex dreams are, indeed, about sex, at other times they are about establishing or desiring intimacy.

Apocalyptic Dreams

Dreams about the end of the world are actually about changes in your own life. They may be reflective of changes you've already made or are about to make, or they may suggest it is time to make a change or that a change is on its way of which you are unaware.

Hi Karen:

Here's my dream: We have a party for a female friend who looks haggard and will not speak with me. Bill and Hillary Clinton are there. He knows who I am. As we go to get food on an escalator, I ask to take a picture with Clinton and my dog and he obliges – and later I will take a picture of Hillary. Instead of using my phone, I use a key fob that I can't get pictures off. When I go back down from getting food, the Clintons are gone (they indicated they would need to leave early) – so I can't get another but I will get it off my fob.

There is a row of flags across the water, and people are going by to place them in flag holders so they stretch entirely across the water. I have a flag that is a cross between Israel and Greece's flag, and I swim to place it in the flag holder about half way across.

~Anonymous

Dear Anonymous:

Thanks for sharing your dream with me. It has several symbols we can look at for interpretation.

First, let's start with the people. In general, people in dreams represent aspects of yourself. So your friend in the dream for whom you've having a party is some aspect of yourself. Because you indicate she looks haggard, it may suggest you are feeling overworked or exhausted. The fact this friend will not speak to you indicates you are ignoring some part of yourself – most likely the part that is causing this exhaustion the first place.

The Clintons are aspects of yourself too, although they may also be associated with an archetype such as the politician or with some aspect of yourself you feel is political. What they represent really depends on how you personally view them.

Now let's look at the symbols:

- **Food** – Food refers to thoughts, ideas, and feelings. Without knowing the type of food, I can't really be more specific than that.
- **Escalator** – An escalator shows movement from one level of consciousness to another (your spiritual journey). So the thoughts and ideas (food) are up the next level of consciousness (escalator).
- **Photograph** – Dreaming of taking a picture suggests the need to focus on an idea or issue
- **Fob** – I'm not really aware of an interpretation for a key fob; however, a fob is a type of a key – just more technologically advanced. A key is a keeper of secrets – or it locks away secrets. So in a dream, a key symbolizes access to ideas, knowledge, etc.
- **Water** – Water indicates subconscious and emotions. The state of the water (clear, cloudy, choppy, etc.) indicates the state of your emotions. Since you don't mention its state here, I can't really comment other than to tell you the water is giving you insight into your deeper feelings.
- **Flags** – Flagpoles represent stability, while flags represent peace and prosperity.
- **Swimming** – Swimming represents exploring your thoughts, emotions, and subconscious.

I think this dream is talking about your political ideals and how they relate to your spirituality. Currently, you are frustrated and exhausted as it relates to politics, and there's even a part of you that's angry at yourself for the current situation. You may be struggling to integrate the two – finding a way to match up a current political situation with your highest and greatest good spiritually. The way to do so exists within your subconscious mind; it's there for the taking when you're ready to find it, even though it feels like a struggle. However, if you continue to explore your thoughts and feelings and pay attention to your deeper emotions about the issues, you will come to a place where you are at peace with current politics and can find a way to balance your ideals with what is happening in the world.

Thanks again for sharing your dream.

~Karen

Chapter 3 – Dream Interpretation Basics

Before you can interpret your dreams, you need to know what to interpret and what is significant in symbolic dreams. The answer is simple: *everything*. The more detail you notice and record, the more accurate your interpretation.

Nothing in a dream is insignificant. If a guy has a beard, it's significant. The color of a person's skin is significant. The number of apples in a bowl is significant, as are the colors, sizes, condition, and shapes of the apples. The context is significant. All of the people are significant. How you feel, what you sense, what you hear, what you smell, what you touch, and what you taste are all clues to the dream's meaning. Even the use of specific words and phrases may be important in a dream, particularly if those words and phrases have meaning to you.

In general, when you interpret your dreams, use the following steps.

1. Start by Asking What You Think the Dream Means

Sometimes, dream interpretation is super easy. I find that many times I know what a dream is about before I interpret it and then when I do the interpretation, I discover it was exactly what I thought it was in the first place. Trust your intuition. If you believe you know what your dream is about, go with that. Your innate guidance is trying to tell you something.

2. Determine the Dream's Context or Setting

The context of your dream tells you what the dream is about. This usually has to do with the dream's setting. For example, if a dream takes place in a school, it might be indicating you need to learn something. If it takes place in a hospital, it may be about your health or healing. If the dream is about fighting, you might feel you are struggling with something. Chapter 4 goes deeply into various types of dreams, which can help you determine what the overarching theme of the dream is.

3. Make Note of the People in Your Dream

In general, people in your dream may represent aspects of yourself, they may (if they are people in your life) represent the person you are dreaming about or some aspect of that person you relate to yourself, or they may represent various archetypes. Even strangers in dreams have symbolic meaning and represent some aspect of self, so it's important you pay attention to the characteristics and behaviors of the people that appear. Notice physical characteristics, like beards, hair and eye color, clothing, or jewelry, as well as how they behave in the dream. Noting these context clues will help you understand who or what these people represent in your dreams. We go in depth into people and archetypes in Chapter 5.

4. List Any Numbers as They Appear

Numbers may appear in your dreams as actual numbers; that is, you may hear or see the name of a number, or it may be a number of objects, people, money, etc. So if you see three soda cans on a table, that is a significant number. The meaning of three is telling you something about the symbol of soda cans. If you ask to borrow money and it's a specific amount, like $53 dollars, those are numbers you need to pay attention to. If there are four women standing on a street corner, that's a number to pay attention to. In general, notice how many there are of things, particularly if that number stands out. Obviously, zero and one typically won't appear as a number of objects, but they may be communicated as a word, or as getting first place, being the first in line, attending a zero period class, etc.

While numbers have typical characteristics, they tend to modify or describe whatever it is there are a number of. For example, if there are two red apples, the number two says something about the apples, which are symbolic of something else. So it's important to note not just numbers, but what the numbers are describing in order to truly understand the dream. I discuss numbers in depth in Chapter 6.

5. Notice and Record Colors

Like numbers, colors tend to provide deeper insight into the symbol which is that color. So a red apple may have a different meaning than a green apple, or an orange dress may have a different meaning than a pink one. If the entire dream is washed with a color or colors, that may speak to and modify the context of the entire dream. If a color stands out in the dream, it is a meaning of greater significance than one you barely notice. The vibrancy and shade of colors is also significant. Darker or muddy colors mean something different than lighter or clearer colors, for instance. We talk about colors in depth in Chapter 6.

6. Notice any Shapes That Stand Out

If the shape of something stands out, it may be of significance, as well. For example, if you see geometric shapes on a wall, or you notice an object has a very particular shape that's unusual for the object, then it may be telling you more about that symbol. Unless a shape is off somewhere by itself in a very noticeable way, it is typically a modifier that provides more information about whatever the symbol it relates to is. We discuss shapes in depth in Chapter 6.

7. Notice Other Symbols and Record as Much Detail as Possible

Symbols in dreams can be tricky buggers. Things are often not what they seem. And while sometimes a cigar is just a cigar, it can also represent all sorts of other stuff. In most dream dictionaries, you'll find multiple interpretations for a single symbol. This is where your intuition and discernment come in. As you look up dream symbols, which makes the most sense for you? Notice which interpretation intuitively seems right and go with that. Virtually everything is a symbol: water, animals, objects – they all have meaning within the context of your dream. Often if you are struggling with what a symbol might mean, when you look at the dream's context, it begins to make more sense. I cover symbols in depth in Chapter 7.

8. Pay Attention to Plot or Action to Pull It All Together

Finally, once you've recorded all of the symbols and cobbled together possible meanings for them, look at how those symbols interact with the action or plot of the dream. What are you doing with the objects you see? How are you using them? How do you feel about them? All of these clues help you pull the symbols together into a coherent dream that provides valuable information. Chapter 8 discusses using plot to pull the entire interpretation together.

Personal Symbols Versus Universal Symbols

Everyone has two sets of symbols that appear in dreams. The first is personal symbolism, and it arises from your own associations with the things you notice in dreams. Your personal symbolism comes from family history, social experiences, emotional experiences, societal influences, emotional reactions, learning, beliefs and perspectives, etc. You may or may not be aware of your personal symbols for things – at least not on the surface, but if you think about an object, what is the first feeling or thought that arises for you about it? For example, suppose your first boyfriend drove a green MG convertible, and it appears in your dream. Chances are, that green MG convertible has personal associations for you, and it's more likely when you dream of it, its meaning is related to those personal associations than any universal symbolism arising from the collective consciousness.

Universal symbols come from the collective unconscious – the symbolism that is shared among cultures or all of humanity. These are the symbols you find in dream dictionaries. I recommend always starting with personal associations for symbols and if you can't come up with a personal association, then turn to a dream dictionary for symbolism from the collective unconscious. When I interpret other people's dreams, I use collective symbols almost exclusively because I don't know someone else's personal symbolism unless they share it with me specifically.

Dear Karen:

Okay so I don't think it's so much a dream as a message that was given to me as I only really remember this one short part which occurred just before I woke up. Here is what it was and what was said to me:

I was having another one of my typical whacky dreams, something about Game of Thrones, *I think, when it suddenly cut to this very clear image of a younger woman, with short dirty blond hair, a light complexion but with some mild acne, blue eyes, and wearing glasses. She looked like an ex-girlfriend. She got right into my face and spoke the following to me. It was very clear, and I knew it was French; "Marin Quan." This was how I heard it but after doing a bit of searching myself, I think the correct spelling is "Maurin Quina." I am interested to see what you make of this.*

-Jack

Hi Jack:

Thanks for writing!

Isn't Maurin Quina some kind of a liqueur???

Okay – after Googling, I see it is actually a liqueur poster depicting a green devil (or fairy) with a grin on its face holding a bottle of absinthe. It's certainly an interesting and evocative poster, if nothing else.

As one who has never seen *GoT* (I know – gasp) – I don't know a lot about the show, but I think it is a fantasy show, right? I doubt it has a lot of significance here, as what you really noticed was the cut to this young, blonde woman who reminded you of an ex-girlfriend. I'd suggest you take a look at what that girlfriend might have meant to you in your life as to why she is the one delivering the message.

Let's look at the imagery from Maurin Quina and the details you saw about the girl in your dream.

- The color green (the color of the Devil in Maurin Quina) actually indicates positive change. It is also the color of the heart chakra, and can therefore signify love, or it may indicate "going green" and being more natural. Alternatively, it can symbolize jealousy, envy, or wealth.
- Absinthe is a green liquor and can, therefore, have all the same symbolism as the color green. It's also associated in dreams with frivolity or foolishness.
- The devil (or green fairy) in the advertisement may be a representation of the Trickster archetype – which is a symbol of duality, of playing tricks, or frivolity, and of things not being as they seem. Alternatively, the devil can represent deception.
- A light-skinned, blonde-haired, blue-eyed woman is often representative of the archetype Divine Child, which represents innocence and goodness. In the Christian faith, this archetype is personified in the Baby Jesus. The fact this archetype has acne shows there may be some flaws or self-consciousness you are associating with this image. Eyeglasses indicates a lack of clear vision.

So after looking at the symbols and the dream as a whole, here is what I think it might be about. It's interesting to me that this "reality" (the girl with the message) interrupted what was essentially a fantasy dream (GoT). So basically, you were being given a message to look past a fantasy you may have and explore the reality of a situation. The dream has a few symbols about frivolity and foolishness. I believe the dream is telling you that all is not as it seems, and that what seems foolish or frivolous to you may actually have a deeper significance. You are not seeing something clearly; you are experiencing something as foolish or frivolous when really it is something that, if you can look at it clearly and allow yourself to truly see it as it is, can bring about positive change in your life or in the world.

Thank you for letting me interpret your very unusual dream!

~Karen

Chapter 4 – Context

A dream's context tells you what the dream is about. Symbols for context can either be universal or personal, and I recommend looking to the personal first. For example, I frequently dream about a doctors' office I worked at when I was in my late 20s and early 30s. Although I haven't worked that job in years, I know when I dream about it, the dream is about my health or healing because I personally associate that office with healing.

Context is typically presented in dreams as either the dream's setting (place) or very specific action. For example, if a dream is set in a house, the house provides clues to the overarching theme of the dream. Likewise, if you are falling in a dream, that provides clues to the dream's context. In general, every symbol within the dream further defines, describes, or modifies the dream's context to give you greater detail as to what it is about.

I shared a few contexts in Chapter 2 when I discussed common dreams, such as flying or naked dreams. These dreams are context heavy so when they appear, you know what the dream is about, and the details and symbols can provide further information about the dream's meaning. Along with the dream contexts shared in Chapter 2, the following context clues may appear.

Airport or Airplane

These tend to symbolize higher goals and ideals, as well as new ventures. So, when your dream is set in an airport or airplane, it might be telling you there is an exciting new project on the way, it might be about a new venture you're currently involved in, or it may be suggesting you start a new venture. These dreams can also symbolize the desire to travel.

Beach

If your dream is set at a beach, it's about relaxing and taking a break from reality. It may also be about the desire to relieve stress.

Boat

Boat dreams are about navigating your emotions. Pay attention to the conditions as you travel in the boat; whether it is bumpy or smooth for instance, which can provide detail about how well you are handling your particular emotional state.

Hospital or Doctor's Office

These dreams are generally about healing or are providing you specific information about your health, including mental, physical, or emotional health. If something is being done to you in one of these settings, it may be about giving up control of your body.

Cellar or Underground

Dreams that take place underground are about your subconscious or things you wish to keep hidden or don't recognize in yourself. If the dream takes place in a bunker or a storm shelter, it may be about self-protection.

Cemetery

Cemetery dreams are generally about grief, particularly grief or sadness you have yet to resolve. While this can be related to the death of a loved one, the grief may also be related to life changes, loss of friendships, a child growing up and leaving home, etc. Pay attention to other clues in your dream to zero in on what it means.

Church or Other Spiritual Building

If your dream is set in a church, monastery, or a similar spiritual building, it's often about your own spiritual development. Paying attention to the details of the church, how you feel about it, and whether you are inside or outside of it will provide more clues. Church dreams may also be about things you hold as sacred in your own life.

Courtroom or Court House

Dreams that take place in court are often about judgment – either your judgments about yourself or others or your fear of judgment from others.

Garden

A dream set in a garden is often about abundance and prosperity. It may also signify personal growth. If the garden is weedy and unmaintained, the dream may be telling you that you aren't paying enough attention to your spiritual or personal growth.

Hotel

Hotel dreams are about personal transitions and changes. They remind you that the transitional state is temporary.

House

A house in a dream represents you, and the room you are in tells you more about it. For example, if the dream takes place in the kitchen, it may be about nourishment and if it takes place in the bathroom, it may be about personal cleansing or ridding yourself of things that don't serve you. Factors to notice include how messy or clean the house is, who is in the house with you, and any other objects you notice in the house. If you are in a mansion, the dream is about wealth and prosperity or social elevation.

Nature

Dreams that take place in a natural setting, such as a park, are about personal and spiritual renewal.

School, College, or University

Dreams set in a school are often about personal growth and learning. They may offer information about life's lessons you need to pay attention to, or lessons that you have learned. If you dream about a school you went to as a child, the dream might be about clinging to the past. If you dream you can't get into a school or you are skipping school, it may be about blocking life's lessons or a general unwillingness or inability to learn.

Store

If the dream takes place in a store, it may indicate the dream is about finding new things or making choices. Pay attention to the type of store and the items you chose for more information.

Vehicle (Car or Truck)

If your dream takes place in a car or a truck, it's about control of your journey through life.

Woods or Forest

A dream set in the woods or a forest may be about new beginnings, or it may be about transitions (which are the same thing, really). It may also denote a desire for a simpler life more in tune with nature.

These are just a few of the many contexts of dreams. Personal symbolism and dream dictionaries can provide more insight into what the dream's setting or main theme might mean.

Dear Karen:

I am at a doctor's office where I used to work. Some crime has occurred there, and it was caused by one of the employees. We've just gotten back some of our financial books from the police relating to that employee. Patients start to come in, and I am scrambling to keep up with all of the requirements on a very busy day there. The number of patients is overwhelming. At the same time, a toilet overflows with stinky urine and feces water flooding the floor of the office.

~Anonymous

Hi Anonymous:

Thank you for allowing me to interpret your dream. It has several symbols in it.

- A doctor's office is a place of healing, so the context of the dream is healing or health.
- Dreaming of an old job represents an old lesson that still needs to be learned.
- Theft indicates a loss of something. In this case, you may feel the lesson that still needs to be learned is lost.
- The very busy office keeps you feeling out of control and overwhelmed.
- All the patients are all aspects of yourself. You may be feeling alone and overwhelmed.
- The overflowing toilet signifies a release of emotions – urine and feces are a product of bodily cleansing.
- The toilet indicates a desire to fully cleanse and integrate with Spirit.

This dream indicates a desire for cleansing, purification, healing, and unification with spirit, but your ego is fighting it. The ego desperately wants to retain a sense of separation, while your spirit yearns for integration. Your ego will make noise as long as you continue to listen to its clamor. Instead of fighting your ego, embrace it and help ego to realize that, even as you further integrate with your spirit, you will retain your sense of selfhood.

~Karen

Chapter 5 – People and Archetypes

There's a tenet of dream interpretation that says every person in a symbolic dream represents some aspect of yourself. While this is generally the case, I believe sometimes another person in a dream is there because the dream is actually about that person. This is especially true if it is someone you interact with in your daily life, such as a spouse, child, parent, or co-worker. Therefore, when looking for clues about the meaning of a person in your dream, you'll want to consider that the person represents an aspect of yourself, or it may be about that person if it is someone to whom you are close. For example, if you have a sex dream about your significant other, the dream could mean you desire greater intimacy with your partner, or it could suggest you need to get to know some aspect of yourself more intimately.

What to Notice

When you encounter a person in your dream, whether it's an archetype or a personal symbolism, try to notice the following about them:

- Hair/eye color
- What they are wearing
- Tattoos, piercings, distinguishing marks
- Any details that might seem "off" about that person
- What they say
- What they do
- How they make you feel
- How they smell
- How their voice sounds

These things will further describe the person in your dream.

Look to Personal Symbolism First

As with all other symbols in dreams, it's important to look to personal symbolism first. When you dream of someone you know, what aspects of that person do you relate to yourself? In life, we tend to see aspects of ourselves reflected in our relationships with other people. For example, your relationship with your child may reflect your unconditionally loving nature, while a relationship with a frenemy may reflect judgment or lack of self-confidence. If the person in the dream is a stranger, or if you don't feel there is any personal symbolism associated with a familiar person that appears in your dream, then look to archetypes and universal symbolism.

When trying to figure out personal symbolism, ask yourself:

- What does that person mean to me?
- What do I feel like when I see or think about that person?
- How do I identify that person in my life?
- What parts of me do I see reflected in that person?
- What is that person's role in my life?
- If I could describe that person in one or two words, what would they be?

Archetypes

Carl Jung believed certain representations of people resided in the collective unconscious that were universal types of characters. Jung listed several archetypes, which may appear as people in your dreams. You can also find archetypal energies from the major arcana cards in a standard tarot deck. If someone in your dreams fits any of the common archetypes that follow and they don't fit within your personal symbolism, then they may represent an archetypal energy.

Persona

The Persona archetype is the identity you project to others. In essence, it is a mask you wear that hides your true self. When you appear as a character in your own dreams (either as the experiencer or viewing yourself having an experience), this is the Persona energy. Interestingly, you may recognize the character in your dream as you even though it doesn't resemble you physically. For example, if you dream you are a squirrel, then the dream is telling you about a mask you wear in waking life that is associated with the symbolism of squirrel (possibly someone who is pursuing inefficient activities that don't serve you).

Shadow

Your Shadow represents all of the aspects of yourself you repress or hide. This may include negative emotions or traits you have disowned. Shadows can appear in dreams in many ways: they can literally be a shadow, it may be someone who has skin that is a darker shade than yours, or it may be a shadowy figure, such as a thief or a murderer. The shadow's appearance often leaves you feeling uneasy, and they frequently appear in nightmares. Shadows in dreams provide information about aspects of yourself you have disowned, or they encourage you to confront issues about yourself you don't want to see.

Anima/Animus

Yin/yang, masculine/feminine – the animus represents the male and female aspects of your personality. Everyone is a balance of energies; nobody is 100 percent one way or the other, and balance between opposites serves a valuable purpose. In your dream, if you experience the anima or animus, it will be either a very masculine (Animus) character – like a Viking or a musclebound beach dude or very feminine (Anima), such as a glittery dolled up movie star or a total girly girl. Anima and Animus may also have some exaggerated masculine or feminine aspect or show a balance of both, like a man in a dress or a woman in a tuxedo. Animus and Anima may also show up with a very specific "feel" to them; you notice their energy feels excessively masculine or feminine, for instance. When the Anima or Animus appears in your dreams, they remind you to create balance between the two and avoid going to the extreme with either.

Divine Child/Innocent

This is an archetype in dreams that represents your purest self – the part of you that is Divine who exists in beauty and innocence. The Divine Child may be represented by a beautiful blonde or cherubic child, an angelic child, or an infant. It may also be you as a baby or young child. When the Divine Child appears in your dreams, it reminds you to embrace the aspect of yourself that is Divine and to allow the innocent and trusting part of your nature to come forward. It may also suggest you are being too trusting or naïve.

Wise One (Wise Old Man/Wise Old Woman)

When the Wise One appears in your dreams, often represented as a helpful authority figure such as a mentor, guru, spiritual leader, or teacher, it is often a sign the dream is about guidance and learning. Pay special attention to dreams featuring the Wise One, because there is much to be learned here.

Trickster

This archetype may appear in a dream as a joker, a comedian, or someone who makes you laugh or look on the lighter side of life. A Trickster may also appear as someone in a dream who embarrasses you by making jokes at your expense or pointing and laughing (like when you're walking naked down a city street or through the halls of your high school). Tricksters in dreams may be urging you to lighten up, or he/she may be showing you you've made an error in judgment that needs to be addressed so you won't be embarrassed.

Great Mother

The Great Mother is the nurturer in dreams. It may be your mother or grandmother, it may be you as a mother, or it may be some other wise, loving, nurturing, feminine presence. The Great Mother often appears to provide reassurance when you are feeling insecure or to remind you to take better care of yourself.

Hero

This archetype is often represented as someone who comes in and saves the day. It can be either masculine or feminine in a dream. It could show up as a fierce warrior, someone you respect, or even your favorite superhero. In dreams, the Hero represents confidence and bravery and often offers solutions to conundrums you may be dealing with in waking life. The Hero provides guidance about how to move forward confidently with self-assurance.

Fool

Similar to the Innocent, the Fool wanders through life's travels and adventures in a state of presence and current-time focus. The fool may appear as a hapless wanderer in your dreams, and he reminds you to remain focused in the present with a beginner's mind – that is, a mind without preconceived notions taking life as it comes.

Magician

The Magician is a cunning creator who uses all of the resources available in life to bring ideas into being. The Magician appears in dreams to remind you to use all of the tools you have available to make your dreams a reality.

Hermit

The Hermit (or recluse) appears in dreams as a person who spends time away from other people. The Hermit (male or female) is a reminder to take time alone and contemplate the spiritual.

Dear Karen,

I'm a pretty active dreamer with several WTF moments. I've been keeping a journal as suggested to help. This last one has me scratching my head, as I believe I have not had one like it before.

In my dream, I wake to find my right leg has been tattooed from the knee down. I'm furious, and the people around me keep telling me to calm down because it's not permanent ink. The tattoo is a series of lines and weird-looking hieroglyphics I could not understand. The only symbol I could recall is a tree with a swirl in the leaves. It was the most prominent item.

So as the week progresses, before I go to sleep I tell myself I need help to understand if this is important and the meaning of the dream. A few nights later, I am walking with a man known to me in the dream but not in reality. I'm telling him about it, and he introduces me to another man. He tells me if anyone can figure it out it would be him. He asks me to sketch it, and he will work on it. So far no additional dreams have followed. I've never had a symbol in a dream before like this and am very perplexed. Any insight would be greatly appreciated!"

~Kelly

Dear Kelly:

Wow — what an interesting dream! It didn't even make any pretense of not being symbolic. In fact, the dream seemed to be telling you its entire purpose was symbolic, didn't it?

I'm guessing the men in later dreams were guides or some aspect of your higher self. I'll be interested to hear if they come back to you after we do some interpretation here.

Your dream has several symbols, including:

- Tattoo
- Tree
- Leaves
- Hieroglyphics – especially a spiral
- Right leg

Let's look at each, as well as the context in which they occur to help you gain insight.

- Tattoos in dreams suggest you are longing to express your individuality or to stand out somehow from others.
- Trees symbolize growth and hope. Legs indicate standing on your own two feet and taking control.
- Spirals represent an inner-directed path to spirituality.
- The right side is conscious reality and deliberate actions or choices. Leaves represent making improvements in your life. Hieroglyphics suggest obstacles to discovering your path in life.

Taken together, the dream is suggesting you are seeking your individual path in life – one that allows you to be in control of your destiny through deliberate choices and actions. While you are seeking to make improvements, you are facing some obstacles, as well. This frustrates you, but your higher self is trying to remind you this present state of flux is impermanent. While you may be frustrated about your current situation, be patient and know you are moving through it into a new beginning. Keep at it! I'm betting as you start to work with these ideas, the two men will return in your dreams and help guide you along your path.

~Karen

Chapter 6 – Numbers, Colors, and Shapes

Numbers, colors, and shapes seldom exist by themselves in a dream (for example, you don't typically see a red haze or a square just sitting in the middle of a room) so in general, these aspects of your dreams tend to provide deeper insight into the symbol they modify or describe. For example, if you have three green bananas, the number and colors of the bananas tell you something about that symbol that would be different than if you had four purple bananas.

Occasionally, you may spot a number, color, or shape all by itself, and when this is the case it means that aspect has a significance all of its own as opposed to modifying and describing some other symbol.

Numbers

Numbers can occur in all sorts of ways in dreams. For instance, there might be a child who is four years old, you might see someone hold up two fingers, there may be a certain number of an object, they may appear as an amount of money, you might hear a phrase repeated three times, you may see a date circled on a calendar, or you might hear a number spoken or see it written somewhere. When a number makes itself apparent in a dream, then it is trying to tell you something.

The field of numerology is complex so I am vastly simplifying it for the purposes of dream interpretation. If you'd like to learn more about numerology, I recommend getting a good numerology reference book, which can help you take your dream interpretation to the next level.

All of the single digit numbers 0 through 9 all have unique meanings. Master numbers are double digit numbers 11, 22, and 33. All other two-digit (or three-digit, four-digit, etc.) numbers are typically a combination of the meaning of each of the numbers that makes up the whole. So 57, for example, would be a combination of meaning of the numbers five and seven.

Zero (0)

The number zero typically doesn't show up in dreams unless you see a "0" written somewhere, it appears as part of an address or phone number, it's part of another number (like 20), or you hear the word "zero" spoken. When it appears in dreams in this way, it can represent several things:

- Nothingness
- Emptiness
- Space
- A placeholder
- Divinity
- Yin/yang
- Totality
- The universe

One (1)

Since in dreams there are often a lot of single things (one person, one bed, one window, etc.), like zero it may need to be spoken, written, part of another number, or obviously highlighted to have meaning. When it does appear in dreams, it may represent any of the following:

- Singularity
- Loneliness
- Ego
- Autonomy

- Individuality
- Leadership
- Originality
- A pioneering spirit
- Unlimited potential
- Getting back to basics
- Simplicity
- Individualism
- Independence
- Self-reliance
- Rebellion
- Stubbornness
- Selfishness
- Weakness

Two (2)

The number two often shows up in dreams as a pair of something, such as twins, shoes, candlesticks, dice. You may also hear or see it spoken, or it may be on money or doing activities in twos. You can hear it, as well, such as hearing two knocks. In dreams, two may represent any of the following energies:

- Balance of opposites
- Partnership
- Yin/yang
- Femininity
- Patience
- Intuition
- Resilience
- Humility
- Qualities that come in twos or pairs, such as happy/sad
- Oversensitivity
- Carelessness

Three (3)

Threes may show up in dreams in the obvious way, such as dates or three of something (three people, three golf balls, etc.). They can also be present in trilogies, such as father-son-holy spirit, body-mind-spirit, past-present-future, yesterday-today-tomorrow, etc. When this energy shows up in your dreams it may represent:

- Vitality
- Inner strength
- Creativity
- Self-exploration
- Exuberance
- Spirituality in the human experience
- Self-expression

- Imagination
- Joy
- Optimism
- Talent
- Extravagance
- Overindulgence
- Hypocrisy
- Impatience
- Intolerance or prejudice

Four (4)

Four is a number of stability and balance. It may show up as a number, an amount of something, or it may show up in things that typically come in fours, such as the four directions (north, south, east, west) or the four elements (earth, wind, fire, water). When the four energy is in dreams, it may represent:

- Limitation
- Stability
- Hard work
- Reliability
- Down-to-earth
- Conscientiousness
- Honest
- Trustworthy
- Methodical
- Stubbornness
- Lack of imagination
- Lack of originality

Five (5)

Five may show up as a number, or as things that come in fives, such as your five senses. The meaning of five in dreams might include:

- Taking action
- Boldness
- Spontaneity
- Daring
- Adventure
- Adaptability
- Versatility
- Curiosity
- Sociability
- Wit
- Carelessness
- Irresponsibility

Six (6)

A lot of people stop counting objects when they get to about six, so it may not show up in a number of objects unless it's very obvious. You may hear it spoken or hear six of something, see a six-pack, or see it written. In dreams, six may represent:

- Cooperation
- Balance
- Nature
- Union
- Bliss
- Perfection
- Community
- Compassion
- Protection
- Loyalty
- Idealism
- Anxiety
- Suspicion
- Jealousy
- Cynicism

Seven (7)

Seven shows up in a lot of my dreams, and it's always been a number I've been drawn to. You may notice the number seven or see or hear seven of something, or it may appear as things that come in sevens, such as chakras or days of the week. Seven energy in dreams may represent:

- Healing
- Completion
- Luck
- Intelligence
- Spirituality
- Connection to a higher power/Divinity
- Wisdom
- Perseverance
- Sarcasm
- Lack of trustworthiness
- Social awkwardness

Eight (8)

Eight is a strong number that in dreams may represent the following:

- Karma
- Success
- Power
- Control
- Intuition
- Insensitivity

- Violence
- Greed

Nine (9)

Nine is another number I am drawn to. My birth calculation is a nine (date of birth with the digits all added together). Nine in dreams might represent:

- Completion
- Closure
- Rebirth
- Inspiration
- Compassion
- Generosity
- Creativity
- Self-sufficiency
- Egocentricity
- Fickleness
- Arrogance

Eleven (11)

Eleven is one of three master numbers in numerology, which are particularly powerful combinations of numbers. If an 11 shows up in your dreams it may represent:

- Intuition
- Instinct
- Innate wisdom
- Charisma
- Anxiety
- Stress
- Lack of focus

Twenty-two (22)

The second master number, if 22 shows up in your dreams it might represent:

- Pragmatism
- Manifestation
- Ambition
- Discipline
- Precision
- Balance
- Impracticality

Thirty-three (33)

Thirty-three is the final master number. In dreams, it may suggest:

- Knowledge
- Understanding
- Humanitarianism
- Mastery
- Unnecessary piety

- Ascension

Colors

In dreams, colors also have significance. In general, they tend to further describe a symbol and help you gain insight and clarity into its meaning. You'll notice colors in all sorts of places – from hair and eye color to colors of clothing, objects, animals, plants and flowers, and more. If a color stands out to you in a dream, it is significant.

Hues

Lighter and clearer colors tend to have more positive aspects, while darker or muddier colors tend to represent the negative aspects of the shade. So a muddy blue will have a different meaning than a clear, bright blue.

Black

Black may represent any of the following:
- Unconscious
- Shadow self
- Unknown
- Death
- Hate
- Hard feelings
- Mourning
- Hidden qualities
- Hidden potential
- First chakra
- Grounding

Blue

Blue may represent any of the following:
- Heaven
- Loyalty
- Truth
- Wisdom
- Calmness or tranquility
- Honesty
- The fourth chakra (throat chakra)
- Open-mindedness
- Sadness
- Speaking your truth

Brown

In dreams, brown may represent any of the following:
- The third chakra
- Earthiness
- Worldliness
- Nature
- The element of wood

- Practicality
- A happy home
- Comfort

Gold

Gold, which represents the third, or solar plexus, chakra may also represent:
- Self-worth, self-esteem
- Cheerfulness
- Spiritual reward
- Determination
- Materialism
- Prosperity

Green

Green, which is the color of the fourth, or heart, chakra may also represent:
- Financial reward
- Healing
- Unconditional love
- Compassion
- Romantic love
- Nature
- Fertility
- Growth
- Jealousy
- Wealth
- Money
- Positive changes

Indigo

Indigo is the color of well-worn blue jeans as well as the third eye chakra. In dreams it may represent:
- Spiritual insight
- Psychic ability
- Divinity
- Protection from higher realms
- Deceit

Orange

Orange is the color of the second, or naval, chakra. In dreams it may represent:
- Friendliness
- Self-control
- Sociability
- Your place in groups, such as family or society
- Liveliness
- New interests

Pink

Pink is associated with the fourth (heart) chakra and may represent the following in dreams:

- Romantic love
- Unconditional love
- Commitment
- Compassion
- Kindness
- Affection
- Joy
- Happiness
- Immaturity

Purple/Violet

Purple is associated with the third eye and crown chakras and may represent the following in dreams:

- Royalty
- Spirituality
- Insight
- Healing
- Devotion
- Wealth
- Compassion
- Justice

Red

Associated with the root, or first chakra, red in dreams may represent:

- Groundedness
- Anger
- Aggression
- Courage
- Energy
- Vitality
- Vigor
- Fire
- Passion
- Blood

Silver

Silver is a color associated with spirituality and may also represent:

- Justice
- Protection
- Purity

White

White is a color associated with the crown chakra, and it may represent:

- Purity

- Divinity
- Higher power
- New beginnings
- Peace
- Perfection
- Angelic realms
- Innocence

Yellow

Associated with the solar plexus chakra, yellow may represent:

- Self-confidence
- Energy
- Intellect
- Illness
- Betrayal
- Deceit

With the colors, remember if they are clear and light (mixed with white), they are the positive aspects and if they are muddy or dark (mixed with black), they are a negative aspect. For instance, a clear or light yellow may stand for self-confidence, while a dark or muddy yellow may indicate lack of self-confidence.

Shapes

Shapes have significance in dreams if they stand out to you or if you notice something has an odd shape, such as finding a phone that is round instead of rectangle. Shapes derive their meanings from sacred geometry, and I'll cover them here briefly since they aren't typically super prevalent in dreams.

- Circles may represent protection, influence, completion, balance, regeneration, or unity.
- Spirals represent the unfolding of spirituality or walking one's path in life.
- Triangles may represent religion, or they may have the same meanings as the number three.
- Squares and rectangles may have the same meanings as the number four, or they may represent stability or materialism.
- Crosses frequently represent Christianity, but they can also represent things that come in fours, like the elements.
- Pentagrams may represent manifestation, femininity, earth, or the wiccan religion.

Dreams from Readers

Dear Karen:

I dreamed I had to use the restroom in my college dorm, but all of ours were in use. I went to a round, tall dorm shaped like a tower because I'd heard a psychic friend of mine was an RA there, and he had a bathroom in his room. However, nobody could show me where his room was, and he wasn't there. Many people tried, like they thought he was an RA too, but he wasn't there. The dorm was pretty dark.

Thanks.

~Anonymous

Hi!

Thanks for allowing me to interpret your dream. I notice several symbols:

- Using the restroom signifies ridding yourself of toxins.
- Dorms are a place of education.
- The round dorm is a tower, which signifies going upward or trying to connect with the Divine self.
- Psychic represents psychic development.
- RA is an authority figure and nurturer.
- Darkness represents unconscious.

The dream suggests you are trying to grow and learn spiritually, but you are feeling there are toxic aspects you need to rid yourself of first. However, you feel like you can't right now so you're trying to connect with your Divine self. I suspect you may be exploring psychic aspects of your personality, but you feel something impure in your subconscious is keeping you from doing so. It may be time to explore your shadow self and integrate the things you feel are toxic into your whole.

~Karen

Chapter 7 – Other Symbols

There are as many symbols in dreams as things that exist, which makes it pretty difficult to come up with a comprehensive list, and this book isn't intended to be a dream dictionary. However, I want to touch on some symbols that commonly appear in dreams.

If you plan to spend some time interpreting your dreams, I strongly recommend purchasing a dream dictionary and/or a psychic symbol dictionary as a companion to the methods discussed in this book. You can also find free dream dictionaries online, although they tend to be of varying quality. The best I have found is DreamMoods.com, but you may find one that resonates more with you. I use three main sources: Dream Moods, *Dream Images and Symbols: A Dictionary* by Kevin J. Todeschi, and *The Book of Psychic Symbols* by Melanie Barnum. Although, I do find myself relying on resources less the longer I work with the dreams.

It's also important to use your intuition when interpreting your own dreams. You'll feel a little click when you hit on the right interpretation, so trust that. Realize that while dream dictionaries can give you a general idea of what the symbols in your dreams mean, it's essential you also examine what those symbols mean *to you.*

Animals

Animals often show up in dreams, and some are more common than others. While animals may have specific meanings, noticing certain aspects about them can convey additional information. Some things to notice about animals:

- Are they wild/feral or tame?
- What condition are they in (healthy, sickly, mangy, alive, dead)?
- What are their surroundings?
- What are they doing?
- Are you observing them or interacting with them?

Bees

Bees represent hard work and industry. They also represent cultivating the sweetness in life. Some other meanings:

- Prosperity, wealth, and success
- Being too busy
- Hornets represent danger, fear, or pain
- Wasps represent anger or negativity
- Being stung by a bee suggests someone has said or done something that hurt you

Birds

Dreams with birds – particularly flying birds – tend to be about your hopes and dreams. It may also represent freedom and joy.

- Hummingbirds represent potential or frivolity.
- Canaries represent happiness.
- Parrots represent gossip.

Bugs

If you dream about a bug, it might be time to ask what's bugging you. Bugs may represent aggravation or anxieties.

- Ants symbolize hard work.

- Beetles represent difficulties in waking life from negative influences. They also might represent self-destruction.
- Ladybugs are a sign of good luck.

Cats

If you consider the personality of cats, you'll likely stumble on what they symbolize in dreams. Cats are feminine symbols, and they also represent fluidity, independence, and creativity. They also may have a literal translation – of someone being "catty."

- A wildcat suggests you are ignoring your feminine side.
- Lions represent courage, strength, and power.

Dogs

Dogs are loyal and protective, and this is what they often represent in dreams. However, the type of dog or the dog's friendliness or aggressiveness may alter that meaning. Likewise, if you have a pet dog and you dream about dogs, then think about what your dog represents to you.

Dolphins and Whales

Dolphins and whales are symbols of spirituality. They may also represent psychic abilities of which you are unaware, or they may be guiding you to trust your intuition.

Horses

Horses represent strength and endurance. A tame horse may have a different meaning than a wild horse; for example, a wild horse may suggest you need to either let go (cultivate your wild side) or calm your wild urges. Think, also, of phrases that use horses in them, such as "on your high horse." A horse in a dream may be a representation of these phrases, as well.

Snakes

Many people fear snakes, and snakes in dreams may be representations of these fears and worries. They may also represent a deceitful person (snake in the grass), or they may be about sexuality and fears associated with that. Snakes might also represent transformation.

Spiders

Spiders may represent deceit, fear, or feeling like an outsider. If the spider is in a web, it might indicate you've worked hard, and it is about to come to fruition.

Blood

Blood represents your life force, as well as your passions and disappointments. To dream you are bleeding may suggest you feel you are giving away your energy or life force or that you are feeling emotionally drained and exhausted.

Buildings

Buildings represent your inner world or psyche. Alternatively, they represent you and your body. Therefore, the state of the building, the colors, the rooms, etc. will give you more insight into yourself. When you have a building dream, know it is your subconscious trying to tell you more about your current state of being.

Clothing

Clothing in dreams relates to the mask we wear or how we wish people to perceive us. It is representative of our public persona. Typically, clothing in dreams is incidental, in that most people wear clothing (except in naked dreams – but that's another subject), so if the clothing doesn't stand out particularly, then it's probably not of importance. However, if you notice a particular piece of clothing, then the dream is drawing your attention to that aspect. Notice things like colors or any slogans or patterns on the clothing for more insight.

Dirt or Mud

Dirt or mud may suggest you want to clean up your act or you're in a dirty or messy situation. Mud might also represent you are feeling unclear about something ("clear as mud"), or that you've been behaving outside of your integrity ("dirty deeds").

Food

Food in dreams tends to symbolize knowledge and nourishment (physical, spiritual, mental, emotional). If you have food allergies or are dieting and you're eating a food you shouldn't have, that may signify anxiety or a fear of lack of self-control. Notice the state of the food (is it tasty? Gross? Stale?) These can all give you greater insight into how nourished you currently feel. Also notice whether you are eating alone (loneliness and lack of support) or with others (sociability).

Nature

Dreaming of nature is about tranquility, renewal, and freedom. Notice other aspects of the nature, such as flowers, plants, animals, sky color, bodies of water, etc.

Vehicles

Vehicles are all about your path in life and how in control you feel of it. Notice, for instance, if you are driving (you're in control), or if it's someone else (you don't feel in control or you feel some aspect of yourself represented by that person is in control). Also notice how easily you control the vehicle – whether it is easy or difficult, how you steer around obstacles, and whether you crash into them. If you crash into an object, notice what that object is because it is suggesting you feel you are on a collision course with some aspect of your life. If the brakes don't work, you may feel something is failing you. If you can't find your vehicle, you may feel as if you are lost along your path in life. If your vehicle is stolen, you may feel like someone else has hijacked your life's path.

Water

Water commonly appears in dreams in various forms: lakes, rivers, the ocean, a mud puddle, a glass of water, a sink filled with water, dripping water. It typically represents your emotions and state of mind, so when it appears in dreams, its state is important.

Is the Water Calm or Turbulent?

Calm, placid water suggests your emotions are calm and peaceful. Choppy water may indicate more turbulent emotions, so water that has turbulent waves or a ranging river may suggest you need to pay attention to some of your more difficult emotions.

How Clear or Muddy Is the Water?

Clear water represents clarity of emotions, while dark or muddy waters may suggest you're having trouble figuring out those emotions.

What Is the Water Temperature?

Cold water may represent colder emotions, while warm water represents kinder, warmer emotions. Hot water may represent emotions that are boiling over or out of control, such as rage or jealousy.

Being in water may represent cleansing (especially if you are showering or washing with water). Being underwater may represent feeling overwhelmed. Swimming in the water may represent self-exploration. If you are out of the water and observing it, you may be feeling detached from your emotions, or the dream may be offering you a way to look at those emotions objectively. If you are drowning, it may suggest you fear being overwhelmed by your emotions. If you are drinking water, it may indicate that you are actually super thirsty, or it could suggest you are refreshing your spiritual and emotional sides.

Dear Karen:

A young boy has done a science experiment that he shows me and two other adults. He has tested four substances in vials, and one of the vials has a top that has turned pink as a result of the experiment. We are excited about that result. As I hold the box with the experiment, some caustic substance somehow gets on my bottom lip and starts to burn it. I wash it away with water on a tissue and it feels better.

~Anonymous

Hello!

Your dream has several symbols of significance.

- A child represents innocence.
- The number two (two adults) represents balance, diversity, and partnership.
- The number four (four vials) represents stability or physical limitations.
- Chemistry represents the need to take chances – or chemistry with another.
- Pink represents love, joy, sweetness, happiness, and kindness.
- Lips represent the need to communicate.
- Burning represents an unwillingness to let down your guard.
- Water represents your emotions.
- Washing represents cleansing and removing negativity.

Your dream is about your relationship with your significant other. It is suggesting you pay attention to that relationship in order to improve your partnership. While the relationship is stable, it could stand some improvement. Adding some chemistry to the relationship (taking chances) can reignite the love, joy, and innocence you once had in it. You need to let down your guard and cleanse negativity associated with the past in order to build a stronger, more joyful partnership.

~Karen

Chapter 8 — Plot/Action and Putting It All Together

Just like a dream's setting or context tells you what the dream is about, its plot is what allows you to pull all the symbols and context together to truly understand what your subconscious is communicating. Plot or action provides the final piece of the puzzle that helps bring it all home.

Just as there are common symbols in dreams, there are also common dream plots that may give you greater insight. Some, such as naked dreams, are so common that most people have them, and they've been discussed previously. The following plot points may occur in dreams.

Alien/UFO Encounter

These dreams may be about feeling alienated, or they might be about seeking a higher purpose.

Being Late

Dreams about being late may be about fears of missed opportunities or time running out, or they may be about fearing change.

Being Lost

If you are lost in a dream, it may be very literal, and you feel as if you have lost your direction in life, or you may feel a little insecure in a new life situation, such as a relationship or a job.

Break-In

A break-in in a dream where someone breaks in to your house signals there is something you have repressed or not acknowledged that is trying to get through to your conscious mind (it's trying to break through denial).

Break-Up

Break-up dreams may be about endings, or they may be about new beginnings. They may also be telling you it is time to end something that no longer serves you; not just relationships, but jobs or other life situations.

Can't Find Car/Stolen Car

If you lost your car or can't find it in a dream, it's about stress and concern about losing your motivation either in general or for a specific project. Context clues and other symbols will help you discover where your motivation is lacking. It doesn't have to be a project; it can be a relationship, a job, spiritual development, or any other area.

Car Accident

Car accident dreams are about fears and insecurities. They may be telling you that you are headed for disaster in a certain area of your life, or they may be warning you to proceed with caution so you don't crash and burn.

Cheating/Infidelity

Infidelity dreams may signal dissatisfaction with current relationships, or they may suggest your relationship needs tending. They may also represent a fear of abandonment (if your significant other is cheating).

Death

Death dreams may be about transitions in your life. If someone you love dies in a dream, it may suggest you wish to cultivate in yourself more of an aspect that person embodies. For instance, if you dream your child dies, it may suggest you wish to have more childish fun in your life, or it may signal you feel like you are lacking in unconditional love or innocence.

Eating

Eating dreams are all about your current state of mind regarding sociability. Who you are eating with (or if you are eating alone) matters here, as does how the food tastes. For example, a dream about eating by yourself and whatever you are eating tastes gross may suggest you are feeling lonely and you don't enjoy it.

Overeating may signify a lack of spiritual sustenance.

Experiment

If you are doing an experiment in a dream, it may indicate you wish to try new things.

Finding Money or Treasure

Finding money or treasure in a dream suggests you are finding something you need, such as a boost of energy or the answer you've been seeking. What you find will give you further clues into what you needed in the first place.

Injury

A dream in which you injure yourself suggests it's time to heal wounds or that you are feeling wounded. Notice where the injury is. In one of the dreams I interpreted in this book, for instance, there is a wound on a baby's leg that a woman's husband caused by shooting the baby. In this dream, the leg means standing up for oneself, and the baby is innocence. I suggested the woman felt her husband had somehow harmed her ability to stand up for herself.

Killing

Killing someone in a dream is about loss of self-control. Alternatively, it might be about killing some aspect of yourself that no longer serves you, such as a bad habit or an attitude. Pay attention to who you kill and what that person represents to you.

Losing Something

If you lose something in a dream, it is often about lost opportunity. Alternatively, it could be you feel you've lost some valuable aspect of yourself. What you lose will give you more information.

Making a Discovery

On the other hand, discovering something in a dream may suggest you are discovering new things about yourself or on the verge of find new gifts. Again, what you discover will give you more information.

Marriage

As in waking life, marriage in a dream is about commitment or the coming together of two separate things to create one harmonious whole. It may also represent reintegrating formerly disowned aspects of self into the whole of you.

Meeting Someone Famous

Dreaming about meeting a celebrity may indicate you are unhappy with your current life and you want it to be more exciting, or you may wish to escape from your current life.

Moving House

Moving dreams are about the desire for change or newness in your life. They also may be telling you that change is on the horizon.

Packing

Packing dreams may represent the desire for change or upcoming change, or they may suggest your life is a bit hectic at the moment.

Plane Crash

Dreaming of a plane crash suggests some of your goals may be overreaching a bit (you might come crashing down). It could also indicate you think your goals and dreams are too big, and you lack the confidence to achieve them.

Pregnancy

In general, pregnancy in a dream indicates growing and nurturing aspects of yourself. It could also suggest you are developing a creative idea, or it could mean you're pregnant.

Trapped

Being trapped in a dream often means you feel trapped in some situation in your waking life, such as in a relationship or a job. Where you are trapped gives you clues to the dream's context.

Traveling

Traveling in dreams represents movement towards your goals and objectives in your waking life, or it may indicate a need for escape from the mundane aspects of everyday life.

Vacationing

If you are on vacation in your dreams, it suggests you need to take the time to recharge and renew yourself.

Wedding

Weddings in dreams are about transitions and new ventures. This may be suggesting you need/desire a new venture, or it may be telling you a new venture is headed your way.

Putting It All Together

The many sample dream interpretations throughout this book should help you see how to put it all together. However, let's follow a simple example here for further clarity using some of the context, symbols, and plots mentioned in this book.

The Dream

I am in my living room trying to use my cell phone to dial the number 1-800-500-0005. I try repeatedly and cannot get my fingers to hit the right numbers. Finally, I hand the phone to my father and ask him to dial. As he dials successfully, I wake up.

Step 1: What Do I Think It Means?

I think the dream means I am having trouble communicating in some way.

Step 2: What Is the Dream's Context?

The dream takes place in my house in my living room. Dreams about houses tend to be about me – either physically or mentally. My living room is where I spend most of my time. So this dream is likely about me and some aspect of my being that is very common in my life.

Step 3: Note the People in the Dream.

Other than me, the only person in my dream is my dad. My dad probably represents the Wise One archetype, which is my inner guidance or wisdom.

Step 4: List any Numbers in the Dream.

1 – Individuality and autonomy

8 – Karma, success, intuition

0 (7 times) – Space, source

7 (from the 7 zeros) – Healing

5 - Spontaneity

Step 5: Notice any Colors.

No colors stood out here.

Step 6: Notice any Shapes.

No shapes stood out.

Step 7: Are there any other symbols?

Only my cell phone. Phones are about communication.

Step 8: Pull It All Together Using Plot and Action.

The plot of the dream is me being unable to dial my phone, and then giving it to the Wise One to dial when I can't. Dreams about inability to use technology like a phone are about feeling unable to communicate.

In this dream, I am trying to communicate information that will lead to autonomy, success, the Source (Divine), healing, and spontaneity. However, I feel I am unable to communicate effectively. The dream is encouraging me to tune in to my inner guidance and wisdom, which will help me communicate and reach those aspects.

Note: I had this dream many years ago (I date all of my recorded dreams) before I started writing books. At the time, I was working a job I really disliked writing technical documentation for industrial automation equipment. It was boring and unsatisfying. I'd been studying, learning, and growing so much in my personal life, and my job chafed. Shortly after this dream, I started writing for *Paranormal Underground Magazine* (after turning down the opportunity once pre-dream) which was the start of all of my current work and communication as a metaphysical writer. The dream was right on – it was encouraging me to take that step.

Dear Karen:

The first thing I remember from the dream is being in my bedroom standing next to my bed. My wife is there standing in front of me. Her hair color is dirty blond and she wears glasses. She is thin and about 5'-9". She is smiling at me, and she has a flip-flop in her hand. She says "here you go" and taps me with it on my right shoulder, and all of a sudden all of these yellow colored baby spiders are crawling out from the bottom of it and onto me, and I am covered with them. I start brushing them off.

They don't hurt me; they are just crawling all over my body. The next thing I know, she turns and walks away, and I am angry at her wondering what she did that for, and I follow her into the living room. During all of this there is a presence in the background watching. I interpret it is her middle daughter and can kind of see her in my peripheral vision.

Now my wife is sitting in her chair still smiling, and I confront her about who she is cheating on me with and she says, "Bob." Then I slap her. The next thing I know I am in Mexico. I don't know how I know that, but I do. It's Mexico, and I am swimming in these caverns underwater, fully clothed along with some other people and a Mexican guide. We are under water, but I can hear him talking clearly. There are some kind of artifacts and treasures around us in these underwater caverns, then we come up into an opening out of the water and enter a scuba-diving shop where everyone is getting wetsuits and scuba, gear, but they don't give me any. Then I woke up.

~Anonymous

Dear Anonymous:

Thanks for writing. That is a really detailed and involved dream, and the fact you remember so much of it definitely makes it appear to be of great significance.

Your dream is rich with other people. If you've read my column, you've probably heard me say this before, but almost always other people in our dreams represent some aspect of yourself. However, sometimes if it is a person in close relationship to you, such as a spouse, it may indicate the theme of the dream is that other person – or some aspect of your relationship to that other person. I'd guess from the context of this dream, your wife indeed represents your spouse.

The setting, your **bedroom**, is the setting of your dream. Bedrooms represent privacy, which are your innermost thoughts and feelings. The bedroom here suggests this dream is about something you keep deeply private. When the dream moves into the **living room**, it suggests that now the dream is telling you about the face you present publicly to the world and how you wish others to perceive you. Finally, the setting switches to underwater, which means the dream is talking about deeply held emotions.

Dreaming of your **spouse** often represents unresolved issues with your spouse in your waking life. This is especially true if there are feelings about your spouse or relationship you are not currently expressing. If you can recall, think about how you were feeling during this dream, and it may give you an idea of what some of these unresolved issues might be. You mention anger, so I suspect you may have some unresolved anger at your spouse.

Flip flops in dreams may be the shoe, or it may be the literal interpretation of flip flopping, or being wishy washy about something. Dreams are like that sometimes. If it is actually the shoe, think about when you wear flip flops; usually they are casual easy wear for the beach, vacation, or somewhere else you are relaxed. Therefore, the flip flops in the dream may indicate you are feeling at ease and comfortable.

The **right shoulder** represents masculine or active attributes, such as aggressiveness, power, or control. It could also be the literal interpretation of "right," as in correct.

Spiders can either represent some domineering female in your life, or it may indicate you are feeling like an outsider. The fact there are so many suggests you feel overwhelmed by and angry about either this outsider feeling or the sheer domination of a female in your life. The spiders are yellow, and yellow indicates betrayal or deceit in a dream with a negative feel.

Here's what I suspect this first part of your dream means. These yellow spiders, of which there are so many, are pointing out you feel betrayed by a domineering female figure in your life, and you are overwhelmed by and angry about this betrayal. The spiders flowed down your right shoulder, showing the act of betrayal felt especially aggressive to you. The fact they are coming from a flip flop is suggestive that you are feeling wishy washy about how you responded to this situation, and that you are still harboring feelings of upset or betrayal about it. Although on the surface you feel you have reached resolution, chances are subconsciously you still haven't, and your dream is trying hard to tell you this.

The fact you are feeling angry and your spouse just walks away suggests you feel she never adequately addressed how you felt about this betrayal, and an observant third party may be you observing the whole thing from a distance and judging you about the incident, or it may be someone else significant in your life whom you felt the betrayal hurt, such as a child. The fact she walks into the living room suggests you feel this betrayal may be out of synch with how you present yourself to the world.

Slapping your wife is the inevitable releasing of your emotions. The slap is telling you that, even if this is something you believe you resolved, chances are you haven't resolved the feelings to your satisfaction, and you need to do some more work – possibly with your wife – to really feel a sense of resolution and to rid yourself of the anger that remains.

The dream changes abruptly here, as soon as you release all those feelings. Now you are in the **water** in a vacation spot. The condition of the water, which you don't mention here, will tell you more about how you are feeling. For example, if the water is clear, you have overcome obstacles and are feeling safe and happy. If it is dark or murky, you are still feeling anxiety about the situation. **Scuba diving** suggests you take the time to delve into your emotions deeply. **Caves** further represent digging into your subconscious and exploring your feelings. Other people represent aspects of self, and people with darker skin (as a Mexican guide would have) represent aspects of your shadow self you still need to acknowledge and explore. The fact they won't give you any protective scuba gear when everyone else is getting it means you feel unsafe and exposed in your explorations, and you may feel other people are safer or more protected than you are.

So, if you look at this dream as a whole, it's meaning becomes pretty clear. You have experienced a betrayal by someone you love – probably your wife. You are still having deeply concealed feelings about this, possibly still some anger and upset, and it's important you delve into them and finally resolve it. While this may leave you feeling exposed and vulnerable, it's important for your personal growth and emotional health you resolve this situation completely.

Hope that helps. Thanks for sharing your dream.

~Karen

You now have all the tools you need to interpret your own dreams. Like the dream I shared in the previous chapter, your dreams have valuable information for you. They can help you understand yourself more fully, and they may help you find ways to bring more joy and fulfillment into your life. The dream I had so many years ago about not being able to dial my cell phone spurred me to tap into my inner wisdom and find ways to bring Light into the world and enjoy more spiritual and personal satisfaction in my own life. Since that dream, I've written more than 20 books and hundreds of articles, taught numerous classes, spoken at conferences, and had the opportunity to share Light with many wonderful and beautiful souls. In fact, that very small dream set me on my current life's path. I'm grateful I didn't ignore it, and I wonder how many dreams my subconscious sent me with the same message before I paid attention.

Your Divine self wants you to live a fulfilled, joyful, meaningful life. Often, the easiest way for your higher self, your guides, or your subconscious to reach you is through your dreams, when your ego is safely stored away and you are in a relaxed and receptive state.

Of course, interpreting your dreams is only the first step. Knowing what your dreams are telling you means nothing if you choose not to act on the information they provide. Once you understand what your dreams mean, it's up to you to make the changes they suggest, embrace the aspects of yourself that live in your shadows, or heal the wounds you nurture that keep you from living your most vibrant life.

Your dreams are here for you. They slip in while you are asleep and provide important, beautiful information. They exist in the dark of night so that in the light of day, you can fly.

The following is a dream a friend sent to me. I mention that only because I am part of her dream.

Dear Karen,

My husband and I were moving from our rented house, and we had decided to leave everything (well almost everything) behind. For some reason, you had arranged for our departure with our landlord.

So on the last day, we were to have been moved out, you and I went back to the house to make sure everything was okay. But when we got there, I kept finding the house filled with treasures I couldn't believe I'd left behind. I kept finding jewels and crystals and glass figurines and a Victorian loveseat, etc. I kept saying, "I can't leave this behind."

So I kept stacking up things to take with us, saying my husband could come and move it for us. But you kept saying the landlord was there and we had to go. We didn't have enough time to move any more things with us.

The one thing I was most upset about was that I couldn't find my travel diary (one I hadn't used since childhood) to take with me.

It was so real and so heartbreaking to leave all those treasures behind.

~Name withheld

Dear Friend:

First, moving and racing to pack/leaving stuff behind is a pretty common dream. I have a recurring version of this myself, which makes it amusing that I appeared in your dream!

Let's start with the symbols and people in the dream. Remember, in this case all people are actually aspects of yourself. So the people in the dream are me and your landlord.

Who I am in your dream would depend on which aspects of yourself you relate me to. So it's interesting that I'm the one telling you that you just need to move on and leave stuff behind. What aspect of yourself (that you relate to me) is suggesting it's time to leave things behind that you no longer need?

These things, to which you hold so much emotional attachment, clearly no longer serve you, and there's a part of you that understands this and is suggesting you move on without hesitation or looking back. I also arranged your departure with your landlord. So let's look at what the landlord might suggest and the part of you that you relate to me is the one who is the catalyst for moving on.

Your landlord is also an aspect of yourself – in this case, the aspect of self that must remain in control. It's your rational side. Here's what I suspect…. you know me as being kind of metaphysics-y/spiritual, so I'm wondering if perhaps I represent your spiritual side. If that's the case, then your spiritual side is suggesting to your controlling and rational side it's time to leave behind things that no longer serve you and move on. You especially want to cling to things from the past and your childhood (travel journal) that you clearly no longer use, but you don't want to let go of any of them.

Spirit is suggesting to your rational side now is the time to let to of these "treasures" from the past. Are they really treasure? Do you even use them any longer? Do they serve you in any way? Your controlling and rational side (ego), however, wants badly to retain these treasures.

The theme of the dream is moving and packing. Moving dreams (and packing dreams) represent a desire for change. You got both symbols, so perhaps you really, really desire change.

The setting of your dream is a house (a rental house, which is by nature temporary). Houses represent the self, so this dream suggests are long for changes in yourself from a temporary state to something new.

There are several objects you mention, as well:

- Jewels represent rising to success
- A diary is a representation of thoughts and feelings from the past.
- Crystals represent looking to the future.
- Furniture represents the desire to please others.

Your spirit is encouraging you that it's time to move forward and leave behind things from the past your ego is still clinging to and retaining. These include thoughts and emotions from the past, worries about the future and success, and your desire to please others. Spirit says, "Let go and move forward from this temporary situation." Your ego, however, wants to retain all this stuff, and it's fighting the urging of spirit with deep emotion because letting go of things we hold on to that no longer serve us can be an emotional process.

In this case, I'm all for listening to spirit over ego, but it's up to you. What are you holding on to, and why? Perhaps it's time to let go of these things (and properly mourn doing so if you need) so you can truly soar.

~Karen

Use the worksheets that follow as you interpret dreams. If you'd like to download more, you can find downloadable worksheets available at: authorkarenfrazier.com/dream.html

Date	3/17/15
Did you ask for a dream before you slept?	No
If yes, what information were you seeking?	N/A
Were you stressed or worried about anything or trying to work out a problem before you went to sleep? If yes, describe.	Yes. I was worried because I had shared credit for a project with someone even though that person had done nothing on the project. That person was insisting in taking all the credit and trying to profit from it, and I felt she was impeding my ability to share my creation freely, among other things.
How did you feel upon waking from the dream?	I felt disturbed and upset when I woke up, and relieved I had been dreaming.

| Describe your dream: | I am sitting with a group of people selling something. We are in a room by ourselves, and I think we are selling jewelry at a long table with dividers on it, but all of our money is going into a common till.

A bearded man is keeping the cash box. A man comes in and asks us for our money. We say no. He goes to a coat hanging on a wall, and he pulls out a round device with a button. He shows me that if he pushes the button it will release some poison gas or neurological toxin.

I tell everyone to give him all the money we have. Everyone hands me the money from their pockets. It doesn't feel like much, but I hand the money to him. I turn to the bearded man and ask if he gave him the money in the box. He tells me he gave him all the money from the till, as well.

The thief goes away with the money, and I contact the police. I go somewhere into a room full of people and tell them we were held up at gun point. One of the people is a friend from elementary school named Brad, who is sympathetic. When I go back to the table, I ask the bearded man if the thief got all of the money from the box. He says it was only part of the money, and that the thief probably wound up with about $37K.

The police have already come and gone. They wanted to talk to me, but didn't wait until I returned. They will come back later to talk to me. |
| --- | --- |

Do you have any sense of what the dream may have meant? What?	The boy from elementary school, Brad, is someone who is in my dreams a lot whenever something major is about to change in my life, so I suspect the dream may be about change.

Main theme of dream/setting (where was the dream setting or what was it about in general)?	The dream was about selling something – which is generally a dream about undergoing change in your life and letting things go.
Were there any symbols in your dream that you believe are represented by personal symbolism? Describe these.	Mostly Brad – as described above.
List the people who were in your dream, and for each person, list what aspects of that person you associated with aspects of yourself, or which archetypes you feel they may represent.	A group of undefined people – all selling something – so all aspects of self that are in the process of change/letting go

A bearded man – represents insight and wisdom

A thief – someone who is wasting my time or stealing my energy or ideas

Brad – change

Police - authority |

Did any numbers occur in your dream? What were they?	37 – so 3 and 7 3 represents ideas, creativity, inspiration 7 represents healing and spirituality
Did any colors appear in the dream? Which colors?	No colors of notice

Aside from numbers, colors, and people, list other symbols that appeared in your dream. Look in your dream dictionary and determine which definitions for these symbols seem the most accurate for you.	Jewelry – self-worth, status, value Table – sociability Divider - separation Money – self-worth and value Till – financial concerns Circle - wholeness Poison gas – ridding yourself of something distressing Gun – anger, aggression, and danger
Placing the symbols and setting in context of what is going on in your life right now, what do you think this dream meant?	I am making major changes in my life regarding my self-worth and how I value myself, as well as making changes in how I interact with others even though I still often separate myself socially. A wise part of myself (bearded man) is in charge of the things I value most about myself. Someone in my life, however, is using my energy and ideas as his or her own and stealing from me. I feel the thief has stolen my creativity and impaired some aspect of my healing. I also feel this is affecting me financially, and I am angry about it. However, it is time for me to assert my authority, which will bring about change in this situation. In other words, this dream is exactly about what I was worrying about before I went to sleep; this project another person had stolen credit for and claimed as her own, and it was telling me to assert myself because it was my creation.

Dream Interpretation Worksheet

Date	
Did you ask for a dream before you slept?	
If yes, what information were you seeking?	
Were you stressed or worried about anything or trying to work out a problem before you went to sleep? If yes, describe.	
How did you feel upon waking from the dream?	

Describe your dream:

Do you have any sense of what the dream may have meant? What?	
Main theme of dream/setting (where was the dream setting or what was it about in general)?	

Were there any symbols in your dream that you believe are represented by personal symbolism? Describe these.

List the people who were in your dream, and for each person, list what aspects of that person you associated with aspects of yourself, or which archetypes you feel they may represent.

Did any numbers occur in your dream? What were they?	
Did any colors appear in the dream? Which colors?	

Aside from numbers, colors, and people, list other symbols that appeared in your dream. Look in your dream dictionary and determine which definitions for these symbols seem the most accurate for you.

Placing the symbols and setting in context of what is going on in your life right now, what do you think this dream meant?

Dream Interpretation Worksheet

Date	
Did you ask for a dream before you slept?	
If yes, what information were you seeking?	
Were you stressed or worried about anything or trying to work out a problem before you went to sleep? If yes, describe.	
How did you feel upon waking from the dream?	

Describe your dream:

Do you have any sense of what the dream may have meant? What?	
Main theme of dream/setting (where was the dream setting or what was it about in general)?	

Were there any symbols in your dream that you believe are represented by personal symbolism? Describe these.

List the people who were in your dream, and for each person, list what aspects of that person you associated with aspects of yourself, or which archetypes you feel they may represent.

Did any numbers occur in your dream? What were they?	
Did any colors appear in the dream? Which colors?	

Aside from numbers, colors, and people, list other symbols that appeared in your dream. Look in your dream dictionary and determine which definitions for these symbols seem the most accurate for you.

Placing the symbols and setting in context of what is going on in your life right now, what do you think this dream meant?

Dream Interpretation Worksheet

Date	
Did you ask for a dream before you slept?	
If yes, what information were you seeking?	
Were you stressed or worried about anything or trying to work out a problem before you went to sleep? If yes, describe.	
How did you feel upon waking from the dream?	

Describe your dream:

Do you have any sense of what the dream may have meant? What?	
Main theme of dream/setting (where was the dream setting or what was it about in general)?	

Were there any symbols in your dream that you believe are represented by personal symbolism? Describe these.

List the people who were in your dream, and for each person, list what aspects of that person you associated with aspects of yourself, or which archetypes you feel they may represent.

Did any numbers occur in your dream? What were they?	
Did any colors appear in the dream? Which colors?	

Aside from numbers, colors, and people, list other symbols that appeared in your dream. Look in your dream dictionary and determine which definitions for these symbols seem the most accurate for you.

Placing the symbols and setting in context of what is going on in your life right now, what do you think this dream meant?

Dream Interpretation Worksheet

Date	
Did you ask for a dream before you slept?	
If yes, what information were you seeking?	
Were you stressed or worried about anything or trying to work out a problem before you went to sleep? If yes, describe.	
How did you feel upon waking from the dream?	

Describe your dream:

Do you have any sense of what the dream may have meant? What?	
Main theme of dream/setting (where was the dream setting or what was it about in general)?	

Were there any symbols in your dream that you believe are represented by personal symbolism? Describe these.

List the people who were in your dream, and for each person, list what aspects of that person you associated with aspects of yourself, or which archetypes you feel they may represent.

Did any numbers occur in your dream? What were they?	
Did any colors appear in the dream? Which colors?	

Aside from numbers, colors, and people, list other symbols that appeared in your dream. Look in your dream dictionary and determine which definitions for these symbols seem the most accurate for you.

Placing the symbols and setting in context of what is going on in your life right now, what do you think this dream meant?

Dream Interpretation Worksheet

Date	
Did you ask for a dream before you slept?	
If yes, what information were you seeking?	
Were you stressed or worried about anything or trying to work out a problem before you went to sleep? If yes, describe.	
How did you feel upon waking from the dream?	

Describe your dream:

Do you have any sense of what the dream may have meant? What?	
Main theme of dream/setting (where was the dream setting or what was it about in general)?	

Were there any symbols in your dream that you believe are represented by personal symbolism? Describe these.	
List the people who were in your dream, and for each person, list what aspects of that person you associated with aspects of yourself, or which archetypes you feel they may represent.	

Did any numbers occur in your dream? What were they?	
Did any colors appear in the dream? Which colors?	

Aside from numbers, colors, and people, list other symbols that appeared in your dream. Look in your dream dictionary and determine which definitions for these symbols seem the most accurate for you.

Placing the symbols and setting in context of what is going on in your life right now, what do you think this dream meant?

Dream Interpretation Worksheet

Date	
Did you ask for a dream before you slept?	
If yes, what information were you seeking?	
Were you stressed or worried about anything or trying to work out a problem before you went to sleep? If yes, describe.	
How did you feel upon waking from the dream?	

Describe your dream:

Do you have any sense of what the dream may have meant? What?	
Main theme of dream/setting (where was the dream setting or what was it about in general)?	

Were there any symbols in your dream that you believe are represented by personal symbolism? Describe these.

List the people who were in your dream, and for each person, list what aspects of that person you associated with aspects of yourself, or which archetypes you feel they may represent.

Did any numbers occur in your dream? What were they?	
Did any colors appear in the dream? Which colors?	

Aside from numbers, colors, and people, list other symbols that appeared in your dream. Look in your dream dictionary and determine which definitions for these symbols seem the most accurate for you.

Placing the symbols and setting in context of what is going on in your life right now, what do you think this dream meant?

Acknowledgments

No work is completed by an author working alone. I always worry I will forget to thank someone, but I do my best. As always I start with my family, Jim, Kevin, and Tanner who are supportive and put up with me when I am in a writing frenzy. Special thanks to Jim for always being my proofreader even though the topic doesn't particularly interest you. I'd also like to thank my friend Jyl Straub for requesting this book a bunch of times before I got on the ball, and my friends Tristan David Luciotti and Seth Michael for giving me a place to teach my classes.

I had a lot of good feedback on cover design and book design from many, including Kristen Gray, Sharon Lewis, Kathleen Marshall, Anna Frazier, Traci Grieve, Jennifer Smith-Brooking, Randy Kovach, Susie Sumpter, Rita Ballard-Baumgartner, and Joe Heithe. Thank you!

Thanks to Cheryl Knight-Wilson and Chad Wilson at *Paranormal Underground* who created such a wonderful platform for me all of these years, as well as all of the readers who have written in to my dream column and allowed me to peer into the world of their dreams.

I'd also like to thank all of the members of my tribe who inspire, support, and share unconditional love, lots of fun, and plenty of laughter. You know who you are.

About Karen

Karen Frazier is the author of several paranormal/metaphysical books including: *Avalanche of Spirits: The Ghosts of Wellington, Dancing with the Afterlife, Pioneer Spirits: Investigating the Haunted Lewis County Historical Museum, Higher Vibes Toolbox, Supernatural: Exploring the Mysteries of the Universe, The Namaste Project, Crystals for Beginners, Hummingbird: Reflections from a Joyful Life,* and *Crystals for Healing*. She also co-wrote *Lessons of Many Lives* with hypnotherapist Melissa Watts.

As a professional writer, Karen has ghost written a number of books and penned hundreds of articles about a variety of topics. She's also a published author in *Chicken Soup for the Soul: Find Your Inner Strength*! *and Chicken Soup for the Soul: Think Possible!*

Karen is a columnist for *Paranormal Underground Magazine.* She currently writes two columns for the magazine: Dream Interpretation, and Metaphysics and Energy Healing. For more than seven years, Karen was also the co-host of *Paranormal Underground Radio In the Dark*, and she formerly served as *Paranormal Underground's* Managing Editor and the producer of the podcast *Paranormal Underground Presents*. Karen is also a member of Spirit Healing and Resolution (SHARe), a collective of psychic mediums and energy healers dedicated to helping people dealing with afterlife experiences and hauntings, as well as offering spiritual coaching and energy healing services.

A frequent guest in media discussing the results of her afterlife research, Karen has appeared on the Travel Channel's *Mysteries at the Museum*, spoken at regional conferences including the Oregon Ghost Conference, Haunting for Hope, Port Gamble Ghost Conference, and Paracon Seattle, and appeared on numerous radio shows. She teaches classes in energy healing, reiki, dream interpretation, and psychic development.

Karen is an intuitive energy healer who is a Usui Reiki Ryoho Master/Teacher (Shinpiden), a Crystal Reiki Master/Teacher, and a certified animal Usui Reiki Ryoho practitioner, as well as an ordained minister for the International Metaphysical Ministry. She has also studied numerous energy and alternative healing techniques including quantum touch, aromatherapy, sound healing, metaphysical healing, and crystal healing. She holds a Bachelor of Metaphysical Science (B.MSc) and a Masters of Metaphysical Science (M.MSc) from University of Metaphysics and a PhD in Metaphysical Parapsychology from the University of Sedona. She is currently working towards her Doctor of Divinity (DD) specializing in Spiritual Healing at University of Metaphysics. Karen is a Nia White Belt who also holds certificates in Life Coaching and Life Purpose Coaching.

Karen volunteered as a Guardian Ad Litem for abused and neglected children, in local classrooms as a music tutor, in the phone room for the local crisis clinic, and at the (haunted) Lewis County Historical Museum. In her personal life she enjoys cooking, hiking, yoga, Nia, and making music.

AuthorKarenFrazier.com

Also by Karen

Spiritual, Metaphysical, and Paranormal
Crystals for Healing
Crystals for Beginners
The Higher Vibes Toolbox: Vibrational Healing for an Empowered Life
Supernatural: Exploring the Mysteries of the Universe
The Namaste Project: Living 100 Days of Divinity
Hummingbird: Reflections from a Joyful Life
Avalanche of Spirits: The Ghosts of Wellington
Dancing with the Afterlife: A Paranormal Memoir
Pioneer Spirits: Investigating the Haunted Lewis County Historical Museum
Lessons of Many Lives (with Melissa Watts)

Health, Wellness, and Cooking
The Easy Anti-inflammatory Diet
The Quick and Easy IBS Relief Cookbook
The Easy Acid Reflux Cookbook
They Hypothyroidism Diet Plan
The Hashimoto's Cookbook and Action Plan
DASH Done Slow
The Complete Paleo Slow Cooker
Acid Reflux Escape Plan
The Hashimoto's 4-Week Plan
Nutrition Facts: The Truth About Food
The Flexible FODMAP Diet Cookbook
The Gastroparesis Cookbook

AuthorKarenFrazier.com